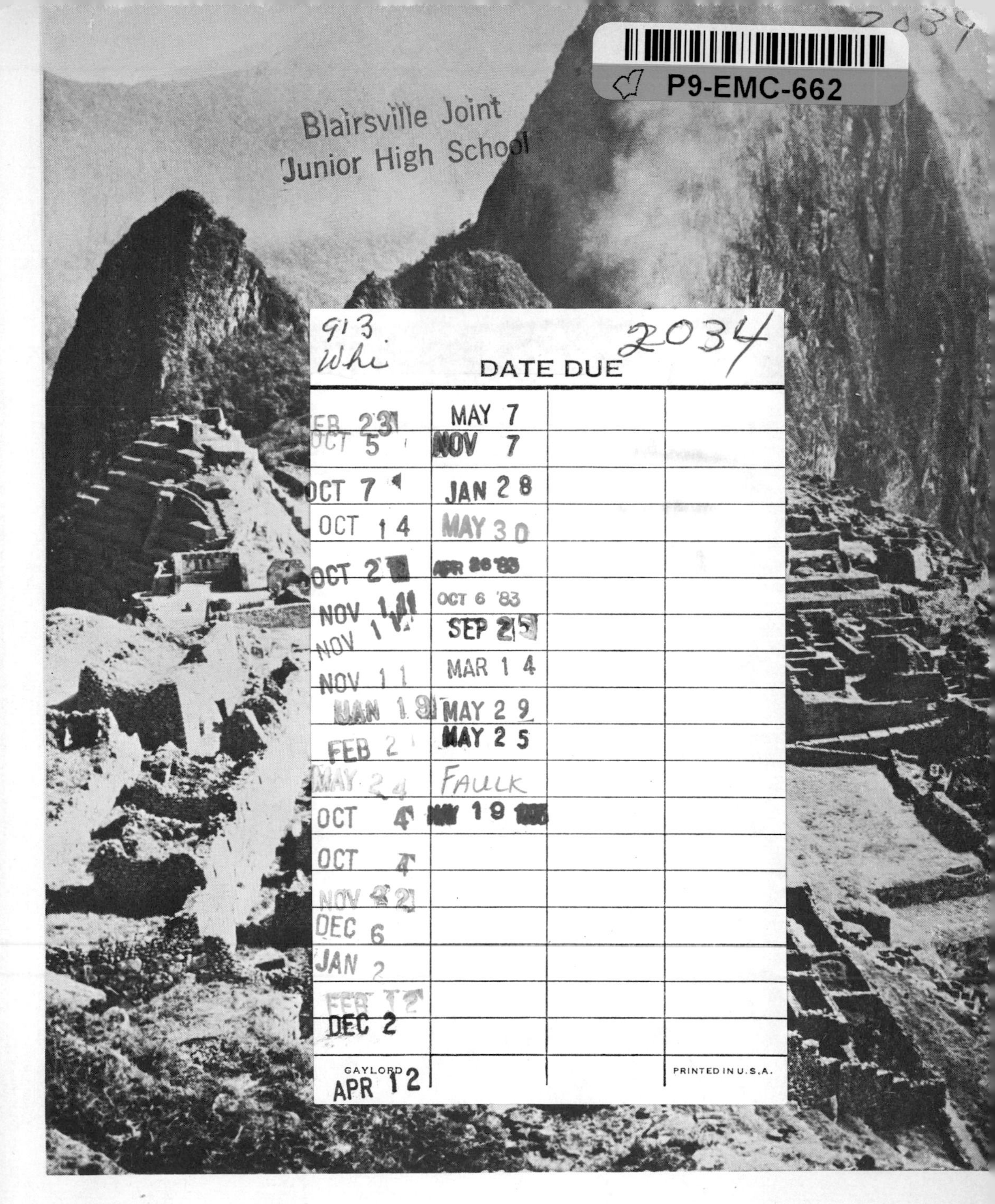

All About Archaeology

The earth is full of the story of man's past—from primitive cave dwellers to the complex civilizations of Egypt and Greece. In *All About Archaeology* Anne Terry White tells how archaeologists have gradually uncovered this fascinating story, and how their remarkable discoveries link the world of ancient man with our world today.

ALL
ABOUT

Archaeology

by **Anne Terry White**

Drawings by

Tom O'Sullivan

with twelve-page photo section

RANDOM
HOUSE
NEW YORK

Published in New York by Random House, Inc., and simultaneously in Toronto, Canada, by Random House of Canada, Limited.

LIBRARY OF CONGRESS CATALOG CARD NUMBER: 59-12363

MANUFACTURED IN THE UNITED STATES OF AMERICA

To Debby,
Judy,
and Suzy

Contents

Acknowledgment

The author is indebted to Frank C. Hibben's *Treasure in the Dust* for the story of the Negro cowboy who found the first Folsom points.

A.T.W.

ITALIAN STATE TOURIST OFFICE

Above: An excavated street in Pompeii, much as it must have looked in A.D. 79. *(See Chapter 3)*

Right: Cast of a Pompeian dog trying to break his chain when Vesuvius erupted. This cast was made by pouring liquid plaster into the hollow left by the dog's body.

WIDE WORLD

WIDE WORLD

Above: Domed tombs in the cemetery built by the Etruscans at Caere. (See Chapter 6)

Below: A revolving flash camera has been inserted into the earth at the end of a tube. This "underground eye" will tell the archaeologist whether or not the relics buried in the Etruscan tomb make excavation worth-while.

COURTESY OF THE METROPOLITAN MUSEUM OF ART

Right: Reproduction of a Cretan terra-cotta statuette of a girl in a swing.

Below: The high-backed stone throne in the throne room of the palace at Knossos. (See Chapter 10)

THE BETTMANN ARCHIVE

The Valley of the Tombs of the Kings in Egypt. The entrance to Tut-ankh-Amen's tomb is behind the low stone wall just to the left of the crates. (See Chapter 14)

BROWN BROTHERS

Howard Carter carefully rolls back the shroud covering Tut-ankh-Amen's second coffin. (See Chapter 14)

BROWN BROTHERS

Members of the Metropolitan Museum Expedition at Thebes (1928-29) sort and put together fragments of granite statues.

Above: Egyptian wood carving of a cat. (About 600 to 300 B.C.)

Upper left: Faience figurine in mummy form, placed in an Egyptian lady's tomb to act as her substitute for any hard work she might be called upon to do.

Lower left: Wooden statue of Methethy, high Egyptian official of the Fifth Dynasty.

THESE THREE OBJECTS ARE IN THE BROOKLYN MUSEUM COLLECTION

BROWN BROTHERS

Above: The famous sphinx at Gizeh with the Great Pyramid in the background.

Below: Archaeologists explore the ruins of a Babylonian temple.

WIDE WORLD

THE ORIENTAL INSTITUT

A painting by Maurice Bardin of a reconstruction of the city of Babylon showing the Tower of Babel. *(See Chapter 15)*

WIDE WORLD

Right: A priceless, 4500-year-old statuette of a Sumerian scribe found by peasants digging a drainage ditch.

Below: This fragment of a wall relief depicts a Mede bringing two horses as tribute to King Sargon II. (See Chapter 15)

COURTESY OF THE METROPOLITAN MUSEUM OF ART

WIDE WO

Above: The tremendous Mayan pyramid-temple, called El Castillo, at Chichén Itzá. Restoration has been completed on the right-hand side. *(See Chapter 17)*

Below: A game similar to basketball was once played on this Mayan ball field. Solid rubber balls had to be pushed through the stone rings high on the walls.

WIDE WORLD

BROWN BROTHERS

Right: Feathered-serpent columns on the façade of the Temple of the Warriors at Chichén Itzá. (See Chapter 17)

Below: A model of the Mayan Temple of the Magician at Uxmál as it must once have looked.

IN THE BROOKLYN MUSEUM COLLECTION

UNITED PRESS

A view of the Incan city atop Machu Picchu, Peru. (See Chapter 19)

All About Archaeology

I

A Piece of Evidence

Back in the year 1926 a Negro cowboy was jogging along on his horse looking for some lost cattle. It was in northeastern New Mexico, and the cow tracks George McJunkin was following led him along a dry, steep-sided gulch. As he glanced up by chance to the far side of the arroyo, what was his surprise to see a line of big jagged bones sticking out of the bank about twelve feet from the top!

George pulled up and sat staring at them. "They can't be cow bones, deep down like that," he thought.

But the bones were big. They must have belonged to some animal as heavy-bodied as a steer. He got off his horse and, opening his clasp knife, began to pry among the bones. Some bits of chipped flint caught his eye. He dug out a couple. They were not like any Apache or Ute arrowhead he had ever seen. The flints that lay in the palm of his hand had straight sides. There was no notch at the end like that on Indian arrowheads. And down either side ran a hollow groove. The points looked like short bayonets.

George showed his find to some of his friends when he got into Raton. "That's not Apache. It's not Ute," they said. Nobody had seen anything like those points before. Who had made them? When?

"It ought to be looked into," was the general opinion.

Word got to the Museum of Natural History at Denver, Colorado, and Dr. Jesse D. Figgins came down hotfoot with some other scientists. They began to dig. And pretty soon the expert was able to say that the bones were those of bison believed to have died out at the end of the last Ice Age, bison with a great head and widespreading horns like those of a Texas steer. As for the chipped flints, they were spear tips. How old, Dr. Figgins couldn't say. But he was very anxious to find out.

Scientists said that Man had lived in America only three to five thousand years. Yet Dr. Figgins believed that those bison had died out perhaps fifteen thousand years ago. If he could find a chipped flint in soil that had never been disturbed and on the same level as the bones, he would know that whoever used the bayonet-shaped points *had lived at the same time as the extinct bison.*

One day the evidence turned up. Before the scientist lay a point embedded in the clay right around a bison rib. Later another one showed up. It, too, was on the same level as the bones. The bison must have been ambushed on this spot.

What an outcry there was! Scientists fought Figgins' evidence tooth and nail. They didn't want to accept Folsom Man, as Dr. Figgins called the unknown hunters, because their flints had been found near the town of Folsom, New Mexico.

"Those points slipped down from the top of the earth somehow," the opposition insisted. "Through an animal hole most likely."

But in the end all the opposing voices died away. There the facts were and they couldn't be disputed. Figgins had dug a new page of history out of the earth.

II

Archaeologists Are Detectives

The finding of a chipped flint indicated that Man must have lived in America for ten thousand years or more. This is how archaeology works. Archaeology is the science of finding out about Man's past from the *things* he has left behind him. Weapons and tools and furniture and pottery, jewels and ornaments, pictures and statues and musical instruments, chariots and wagons, buildings, monuments, roads, canals, post holes—all these are things. The plants Man grew are things. The bones of animals he domesticated are things. A reindeer bone broken by Man so he could suck out the marrow is a thing. So is a sea shell found in a cave far from the sea, where Man has carried it.

Of all the sciences archaeology is perhaps the most appealing. For archaeologists are in fact detectives, and we all have something of the detective in us. We like to work out puzzles and solve mysteries—which is what archaeologists do. They find clues and follow them, then reconstruct what happened and try to interpret its meaning. They try to find out the way our ancestors lived—how they got their food and built their houses and worked and fought. They try to learn about their skills, their trade, their travels, their fun. Above all, they want to get at the mind and spirit of Man. What did our dead-and-gone ancestors believe? What did they feel? What did they imagine?

Take, for instance, the animal paintings on the walls and ceilings of Prehistoric Man's caves. Archaeologists weren't content merely with discovering the fact that Cro-Magnon Man was a great artist. They asked: "*Why* did he paint and engrave pictures of animals at all?" It surely wasn't to decorate his home. For he put the pictures in places where it was pitch-dark, where they wouldn't be seen, in chambers he didn't live in. He put them on without order or arrangement, sometimes one on top of another.

Clearly Cro-Magnon Man wasn't after beauty—beauty

was just a by-product because he happened to be an artist. It looked rather as if the idea was to get in as many animals as possible. There wasn't much good space. So he came back again and again to use the same space.

But what did he need all the animals for?

The archaeologists turned the problem over in their minds. It must be that Prehistoric Man was making magic. Like primitive people everywhere, he must have believed that if you imitate what Nature does you will cause Nature to do that thing: If you make a big noise and wave a burning stick and pour water on the ground, you will get thunder, lightning, and rain; if you make pictures of the animals you use for food, Nature will produce those animals and give you good hunting.

Magic was obviously the answer. It made all the pieces of the puzzle fall into place. Of course the pictures had to be in the dark—isn't the dark the best place to practice magic? Order and arrangement didn't matter. The whole idea was to draw and paint and engrave all the animals he possibly could. Then surely the hunting would be good.

Archaeologists follow clues. In general, they go about it like the great detective in the mystery thriller. But

Prehistoric Man painted these animals to make magic.

they have a much harder job. For the mystery story detective comes on the scene of the crime soon after it happens. All the evidence is there, fresh, entire. His job is merely to pick it up and put it together. But the archaeologist comes on the scene hundreds or even thousands of years after the event. Moreover, his evidence is much more baffling. It is by no means whole and entire, for most things are very perishable.

Everything made of wood, leather, wool, linen, grass, hair, and materials like that turns to dust in a few centuries—or sooner. As for food, except under very special conditions, nearly all of it quickly decays. So all the archaeologist usually has to build his case on is bits of stone, bone, metal, pottery, and glass. He finds axheads, but the handles are gone. He finds hinges, but the doors have turned to dust. He finds post holes, but there aren't any posts in them. He has to labor to make sense out of his evidence. He has to use his special knowledge. And he has to bring to bear on his find such evidence as has been discovered in other places. There have been many lucky finds. Deserts and peat bogs and frozen earth have kept even highly perishable things fresh and whole.

Archaeologists have a harder problem than the detective, but they do have one advantage. They don't have to be in a hurry. An archaeologist can take years to make up his mind. And if he comes to a wrong conclusion, he can correct it later on—or somebody else can.

III

Archaeologists Dig

There is one word that everybody thinks of when he thinks of archaeology. That's *digging*. Of course our ancestors have left some things that we don't have to dig for. There is Stonehenge in England, for instance, that mysterious circle of gigantic stones whose meaning archaeologists try to solve. There are the cave paintings. There are the pyramids. But most archaeologists have to dig.

Now why do they have to?

It is easy to see why they have to when they are looking for things in a grave. Those things were buried on purpose and must be dug for. But how is it that houses and villages and even great cities are dug up from under the earth? How have they disappeared from sight?

One reason why archaeologists have to dig is that in many parts of the world when a building goes to pieces and falls down it soon gets covered up and disappears. Almost at once weeds begin to grow over the ruin. Grass and other plants spring up. Season after season the dead growth mixes with dust and makes soil. The covering of soil gets thicker and thicker. And after hundreds of years there is no building to be seen. It is lost, forgotten. It lies at last several feet underground.

Generally, however, when a house falls down, it isn't left alone very long. People come and cart away the bricks and stones to use somewhere else. Or someone decides to build on the same spot again. He levels off what is left of the first-floor rooms, fills them in, and builds his house on top of the fill.

This has happened over and over again. Sometimes in a modern city in Europe workmen start digging a subway or some other public work. Far down under the city streets they come on the ruins of a building. Thus in the year 1954 workmen came upon a building deep down under London's streets. It was a temple built by the Romans who once ruled Britain.

In Rome, they say, you can go into a church that is a thousand years old. Then by a hidden stairway you can go down into what is left of another church under it. From that church there is also a stairway leading down. It goes down to a house and a temple still older. This house and temple once stood at ground level. Now the streets of Rome are many feet above. Yet this is nothing compared to some of the older cities. At Eridu in Mesopotamia the ruins of fourteen temples have been unearthed, one above the other.

Level it and build on top. That has been the rule. The ground level of many great cities has grown higher and higher as old buildings were razed and new ones built on top. London is thirty feet higher than it was once. A sort of hill has grown up that wasn't there before.

Sometimes after this has happened and an old city has been destroyed—by enemies, say—the spot is abandoned. What happens then?

Slowly what remains of the city crumbles. Weeds grow up and choke the ruins, mix with the fragments of stone and brick and turn to soil. A blanket of soil covers everything. And a grass-covered mound is left, an artificial hill. That's all. Even the name of the city has

A grassy mound may cover the ruins of a once-proud palace.

been forgotten. Shepherds feed their flocks on the slopes. The shepherds have no idea that under their feet lie ruins that once were proud temples and palaces and monuments, homes and busy streets, gates and walls and towers.

Sometimes wind-blown sand hides the works of Man from sight. When the lower part of the Great Sphinx of Egypt was excavated, it came as a surprise to most people that the creature had huge paws. As for the smaller sphinxes, many of them were lost altogether until the archaeologist Auguste Mariette dug them up. He was traveling through the desert one day when he noticed the head of a sphinx sticking up out of the sand. He got down and searched all around. There was a tablet! On it was an inscription saying that the sphinx was dedicated to the sacred bull of Egypt—Apis.

Mariette was a scholar, and he understood right away. This waste land was the ancient cemetery where with great religious ceremony the Egyptians had buried their sacred bulls. He had read in an old book that that cemetery had an avenue of sphinxes leading up to a temple. He must be standing right over that avenue! Quickly he got a handful of men together and set them digging. In an avenue 600 feet long, he dug up 141 sphinxes and the bases of several more. The sphinxes that had stood on the empty bases had been stolen to decorate the gardens of officials in Cairo and Alexandria and Gizeh.

Sometimes land sinks and buries Man's dwellings. This happened on a large scale to the prehistoric peoples who had built their homes out over the Swiss lakes. They had moved there for the sake of protection from wild animals and wilder men. But now year by year they found the water rising a tiny bit around their homes. Finally it got so high that the Lake Dwellers had to move away.

For thousands of years the lake kept the secret of that ancient people. Then in 1853 and '54 there was a drought in Switzerland. The water in Lake Zurich got very low. One day to their astonishment people saw posts sticking up out of the water—rows and rows of them. What in the world did they mean? Who had driven the piles into the lake bottom? Archaeologists began to explore. Houses, they discovered, had once stood on those piles. Four thousand years ago a mysterious farming people had built a village out over the lake. And not only over Lake Zurich but over most of the lakes of Switzerland.

By dredging the bottoms, the archaeologists were able to piece together the whole lost life of the forgotten Lake Dwellers. The peat that had formed at the bottom of the lake had preserved everything. They dredged up wooden bowls and dippers and knives and combs. They rescued bits of linen cloth and cord and straw matting, knitting needles and pins. They got bones of oxen and goats and sheep and pigs. They retrieved all kinds of

The Lake Dwellers built whole villages over the water.

other food—from barley to tiny apples cut in half and dried for winter use.

In tropical and semitropical lands where there is much rain and plants seem to shoot up a foot a night, the jungle has swallowed the works Man left behind him. Vines have twisted themselves about monuments and pulled them down. Soil has collected on the abandoned temples and palaces. Grass, bushes, and trees have sprouted all over the outside. The roots go so deep into the buildings that archaeologists often dare not dig them out lest they destroy too much.

Once in a great while a volcano erupts and buries the

works of Man. There are Indian ruins in Mexico that lie half buried in lava. It doesn't happen often because people have more sense than to build near an active volcano. But sometimes they are mistaken—they think a volcano is dead when it is only sleeping.

In the year A.D. 79 a terrible disaster happened on this account in Italy. Two cities—Pompeii and Herculaneum—were buried from sight. After a sleep of a thousand years Vesuvius suddenly woke up. It began to shower down stones and ashes and let out a cloud of poisonous gases. Thousands of people in Pompeii perished. For eight days and nights the ashes fell. They filled the streets and covered the houses of Pompeii. They buried the city. Then down the mountainside poured a torrent of mud. It was ash from the volcano mixed with underground water. It made straight for Herculaneum. It flooded the city. It seeped into the houses, filled them, covered them. It swallowed the city.

Years passed. Gradually people carried away all that showed above the ashes. Weeds grew over the buried towns. In time everything disappeared. Soil formed. Farmers planted grapevines over what had been Pompeii and Herculaneum and people forgot there ever had been cities there. Even their names were forgotten.

Then in the year 1738 the Queen of Naples decided she wanted some more antique statues for her gardens. Just such statues, she was told, had been dug out of a shaft at the foot of Mount Vesuvius. The Queen set diggers to work there. In a little while Roman statues came to light. Part of a bronze horse appeared. A flight of stairs was discovered. And then a theater. A marker said that this "Herculanean Theater" had been built by one Rufus at his own expense.

Slowly the light broke. The lost city of Herculaneum lay under the diggers' feet! Yes, of course. The old records said that long ago Vesuvius had erupted and buried Herculaneum and Pompeii.

People began to dig. They found the villas and shops and streets, the inns, the temples, the barracks, theaters, and baths. Everything was just as it had been in the year A.D. 79, sixteen and a half centuries before. The calamity had fallen so suddenly that there had been no time to put anything away. The suckling pig was left roasting in its bronze pot. The bread was left baking in the oven.

The earth is full of Man's story. Some of the most precious pages have been buried by Man himself, while others have been hidden from sight by time, or Nature, or both. So archaeologists must dig.

IV

Boucher de Perthes

A couple of times in this book you have come across the words *Prehistoric Man*. Please look at the chart below and you will see just what we mean by that.

↓

5,000

1,000,000 Years *Years*

That line represents the time Man has lived on earth —roughly a million years. Almost at the very end of the line there is a little arrow. It marks off the point in Man's career at which he invented writing and began to leave written records. That date is about 5,000 years ago. The speck of line to the right of the arrow represents Historic Man. All the rest of the line represents

Prehistoric Man—Man before he left any written records about himself.

Now you see at a glance that the prehistoric period is very much longer than the period of written records. But it is only a little while since archaeologists learned that. Only recently did they come to appreciate what a sizable job they have on their hands. For up to just about a hundred years ago people in Europe and America—both scientists and ordinary folk—had a very different idea about Man's time on earth. A century ago nearly all of them believed that Man had been created in 4004 B.C. This didn't leave much time for prehistory.

The person who changed the time scale was a Frenchman by the name of Boucher de Perthes. He was a customs house officer, the son of a botanist, and a man of independent mind. That independent mind of his refused to believe that Man was created in 4004 B.C.—on October the 23rd at 9.00 A.M. to be exact. He believed that Man had lived on earth much longer and that he had had very humble beginnings. Before he learned to use metals, Boucher de Perthes thought, Man had used stone for his tools and weapons. "Those stone implements must still be around—somewhere," he told himself, "and I will find them."

But where should he look?

One evening in the year 1828 he was standing at a gravel pit in his home town of Abbéville when an idea struck him. "Rivers," he said to himself, "overflow their banks. If Man of the Age Before Metals left any of his tools and weapons near a riverbank, they would have been washed into the water. Then later they would have been deposited, along with the pebbles and sand the river carried, in some such place as this."

He stooped down quickly. He picked up one frag-

De Perthes searched a hundred places without success.

ment and another. He picked up dozens, hundreds. To his disappointment, not a single stone showed a trace of Man's hand upon it. Not one had been intentionally chipped into the shape of a tool or weapon.

But he didn't give up. In the years that followed he searched a hundred places, always in vain. Then at last one day in a river deposit right near his own house he found what he was looking for. It was a six-inch piece of flint. Two chips had been struck off it.

He took it to an archaeologist.

"This is the work of Nature, not Man," the archaeologist said.

Boucher de Perthes took it to another archaeologist.

"It is an accident," the other said.

But Boucher de Perthes clung to his idea. And soon afterward he found another flint. It was of the same shape as the first. Then he found a third. It, too, was shaped like the others.

"Doesn't this show that man fashioned them?" he asked the archaeologists.

"No," they replied. "It is just an accident of Nature."

Boucher de Perthes' answer was to hire laborers to help him find more flints.

One day a workman brought him a piece of stone he

had taken from the river drift. Anyone could see it was a hatchet. But more important was the fact that it had come out of a spot never touched before—thirty feet from the surface. From just such a level huge animal bones had recently been taken. They had proved to be the bones of elephants and rhinoceroses. The flint hatchet, then, was as old as the bones. The man who had chipped that hatchet had lived perhaps a hundred thousand years ago—when elephants and rhinoceroses were walking around France!

Boucher de Perthes hurried to his archaeologists.

"Yes, it is a hatchet," they admitted. "But it didn't come from where you say it did. It couldn't have."

The customs officer went on looking for flints. Year after year he searched. And he got what he wanted. It had taken him almost ten years to find his first four flints. In the next nine he got so many that he had to build a gallery onto his house to hold them. It was a strange museum, the only one of its kind on earth. It held nearly all that the world knew of the Stone Age. Whoever came in could see Man's whole upward climb. There were his first rough strokes on flint and stone. There were all the slow steps up and up to polished, keen-edged flints, saws, knives, hammers. The visitor could see stone hatchets with handles of stag horn. He could see boxes carved out of the kneecaps of oxen. He could see javelins fashioned from bones hardened in the fire.

But Boucher de Perthes wasn't satisfied to have his things viewed just by the folk of Abbéville and the rare strangers who passed through town. He wrote to a Paris museum and offered his entire collection free.

The museum didn't want it. Paris didn't believe in his Age of Stone. His collection was a fraud.

Boucher de Perthes sat down and wrote a book about Man of the Stone Age and sent it to the Academy of Arts and Sciences. The book looked so impressive that many of the gentlemen read it. But what he said upset everything that science and religion taught. So they shut their minds.

It looked as if the case for Man of the Stone Age was closed. And doubtless a good many more years would have passed before he came into his own had it not been for a happy chance. A famous British scientist passed through Abbéville in the year 1858. He had read Boucher de Perthes' book and took the trouble to look in on his museum. Hugh Falconer's specialty was prehistoric animals. It was said that if you gave him a single tooth, he could draw the rest of the animal for you.

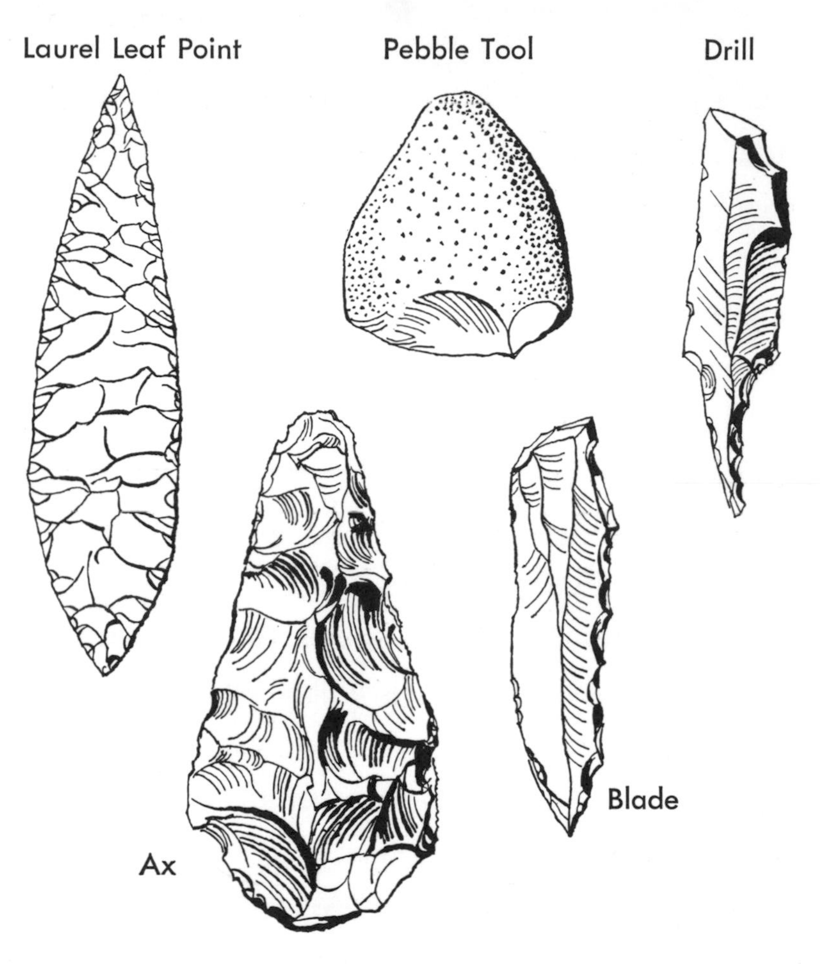

Five types of stone implements.

The scientist entered the museum and looked around in amazement. He was swept off his feet by the convincing proofs that Man had lived in France at the same time as the extinct elephant, rhinoceros, and hippopotamus. He spent the whole day in the museum and that same night wrote to his geologist friend Joseph Prestwich. "If next summer you should happen to be paying a visit to France," he said, "let me strongly recommend you come to Abbéville. I am sure you will be richly rewarded."

Prestwich didn't wait till summer. The question of how long Man had lived on earth was bothering him too much. Within a few months he crossed the Channel, and was as solidly convinced as Falconer.

Back in England, Prestwich addressed the Royal Geological Society and created such a sensation as had not been seen in those rooms for years. Many a member's lifelong views were shaken. For Man of the Stone Age couldn't be dismissed just like that if the great Joseph Prestwich went to bat for him. Created in 4004 B.C.? No indeed. Man had suddenly leaped back. He stretched back so far that his beginnings were lost in a haze.

Before his lecture Prestwich had laid some flints out on a table. At the end of his talk he swept his hand over them. "Here," he said, "are the instruments worked by the hands of Man, discovered in the depths of the globe."

The gentlemen crowded curiously around to see.

V

The Oldest Burial in the World

Several caves had been explored even before this time, but now archaeologists went in armed with new understanding. Digging down into the cave floors or into the terraces just outside, they found the tools and weapons of various kinds of Prehistoric Man. Sometimes they even came upon his bones.

More often than not it was the earth just outside the entrance that yielded up the most. For the Cave Men had lived less in the cave than on the terrace outside. It was too dark in the cave for them to work. Moreover, they could make a fire on the terrace and cook, and the smoke didn't choke them. In pleasant weather they could feast in the open. Here the women brought the hides to scrape and soften and make into clothing. Here the men worked their ivory and horn. Here in the light and fresh air they shaped their tools of flint.

Waste flakes fell by the thousand on the terrace. Worn-out and broken flints littered it. And even perfectly good tools often got lost in the tricky floor. In those days people weren't bothered with our notions of cleanliness. They never took the trouble to sweep. They never "picked up." They let litter lie where it fell. They stepped on it and trampled it down into the floor. Generation after generation and century after century the trash gathered until the Cave Men lived on top of what we would call a dump.

That is what made it so fascinating to excavate a terrace—or a cave. The archaeologists would sink a trench to study the dump. When the trench was dug, they could look up and see the layers—just as in a layer cake, but uneven in size with the frosting sometimes thick and sometimes thin. The oldest layer, of course, they knew would be at the bottom and the newest at the top. Common sense told them that. Just as with a pile of books, the one at the bottom had to be the one that was laid down first.

Perhaps the very top layer would be sterile—have

nothing in it, that is—and yet it might be several feet deep. But that had its own story to tell. The archaeologists realized that all the time the top layer of dirt was gathering, no one had lived on the dump. Next they might come on a layer that had in it the bones of animals still common today and also bits of pottery. They would know then that men living near the age of polished stone had occupied the cave. For Cro-Magnon Man had no pottery. Perhaps the next layer would have long, narrow worked flints in it and objects of reindeer horn and bones of mammoths. The archaeologists would recognize this as a layer belonging to Cro-Magnon Man. The layer below might be sterile again, showing another period when nobody lived in the cave. Under that perhaps there would be a layer containing flints of a type that had come to be known as those which Neanderthal Man had used. Along with them there would be sure to be bones of extinct animals—the woolly rhinoceros, most likely, and the mammoth. And below that there would be nothing more. They would be down to virgin soil.

The explorers would go home and write up their notes and report on what they had found. Each layer with things in it they reported as an *occupation layer.*

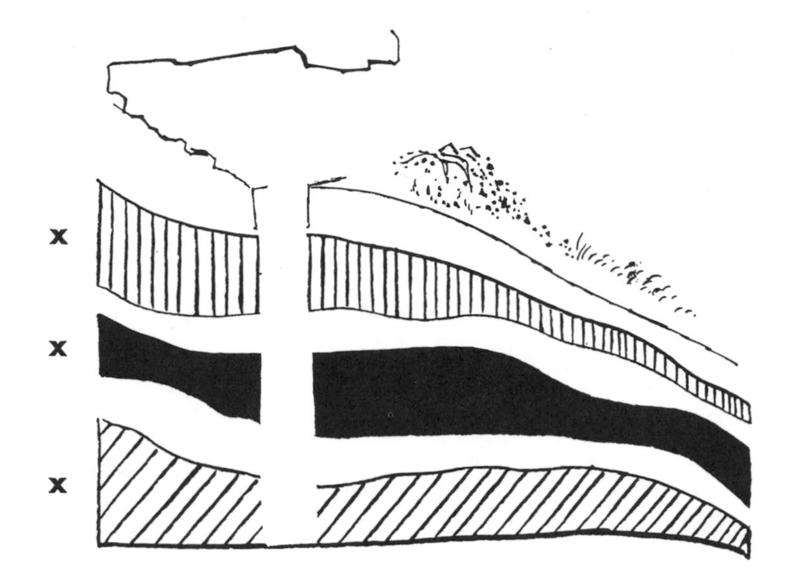

Diagram of a trench cut through the occupation layers of a shallow cave floor. X's mark the layers of occupation.

That is, a period when the site was occupied, or lived on. Each occupation layer represented what they called a *culture*. And by that word they didn't mean *refinement*. They meant *a way of doing things*. They would describe just how one culture followed another on the site. And before they had done, they had given a picture of the whole *sequence of cultures*. This would be added to everything else that was known about the Cave Men. And little by little a clear picture of what they were like would be built up.

The names Neanderthal Man and Cro-Magnon Man

got to be very familiar to the scientists, but ordinary folk as yet hardly knew the words. Then came the news about the paintings and drawings and engravings on cave walls and ceilings. By 1905 it was pretty well known that Cro-Magnon Man was not only tall and beautifully formed but that he had been a great artist. As for ugly little Neanderthal Man, he was still a question mark in some respects. Archaeologists had shown that the caves had belonged to him first, and also that he had been a man of courage. For had he not driven out the cave lions and the fierce cave bears to get a home for himself? Had he not hunted the huge mammoth and the woolly rhinoceros? But what sort of person he had been besides was a puzzle. Were there any complicated thoughts in that big head of his with the heavy ridges of bone above the eyes? Thoughts about something besides food and shelter?

In the year 1908 three French priests—the Abbés A. and J. Bouyssonie and L. Bardon—dug up the answer to that question.

They had chosen to explore a cave in the south of France, just outside the village of La Chapelle-aux-Saints. It was very small as caves go—only nineteen and a half feet long. The roof came down low. They could see that they would at no time be able to stand up straight inside. And as the cave was filled with dirt and fallen rock almost to the roof, they would have to do all their work at the start on hands and knees. But the flame of archaeology burned strong in them and they commenced.

Almost at once they understood that they were on the trail of Neanderthal Man, for all of the flints which they dug up were of the type he had made. All the animal bones were of such beasts as he had hunted. No one had lived in the cave after his time. And as the priests dug down and down they saw that nobody had lived there before him. After three years of digging and scraping and sifting, they had quite a little collection, all of it illustrating the life and times of Neanderthal Man.

It was now August, 1908. They were down to the hard cavern floor. "Just a little longer and we can sit down at ease and write up our notes," they thought.

Then on the third day of the month they noticed a break in the cave floor. They threw their lights on the spot, passing their hands over it again to make sure. No question about it, there was a ditch here. It had been purposely dug, and afterward filled in, by some person or persons in the time when the mammoth and rhinoceros roamed Europe. Could there be any doubt what a hole in such a place would have been dug for? It must be a grave. If so, the bones of a human being, of Neanderthal Man, lay directly under their feet!

Feverishly they began to move the soil. In a little while they could see that they had guessed right. The skeleton was there. They were looking on the oldest known burial in all the world!

The skeleton lay on its back, the head to the west. The left arm was stretched out, the right bent so that the hand lay near the head. Both legs were partly bent. Around the head was a row of stones, while all about lay worked flints and bits of ocher. Several large flat pieces of the long bones of animals lay about the skeleton, indicating that food had been provided for the dead. And near the head lay the foot bones of a great ox or bison.

The three men examined the skeleton with awe. It was that of a grown man—later they would know he was perhaps fifty or fifty-five. He was short. And he had a very large head. His eye sockets were very deep and wide, and above them were enormous ridges of bone.

What had he done, this unknown man, to have deserved such honors at his death? Was he a leader in the chase? A wise head at the council fire? Or simply a father loved and mourned by his hunter sons?

It was a mystery which could never be solved. But one thing the priests were sure of. They had caught a glimpse of the thoughts that had once gone on in that monstrous skull. This Neanderthal Man and those who had laid him to rest so honorably had risen far, far above the beast. They had imagination. Their thoughts had wings. Like the Egyptians, like the American Indians, these men of perhaps 130,000 years ago had believed in a spirit life beyond the grave. That was the meaning of the food offerings and the tools placed near the body. They were to sustain and help the spirit in that after-life.

The thought somehow brought the Neanderthal Man very close to the priests. The thousands of years slipped away as they looked at the grave. Their common faith linked them in a sense of kinship with the dead.

VI

Out of Etruscan Tombs

For five thousand years Man has been leaving his written records behind him. You might suppose that archaeology would let Historic Man pretty much alone since he speaks for himself. But not at all. Archaeology is just as much interested in Historic as in Prehistoric Man. For even in the time of written records, *things* often have more to say to us than words. Some of the records have been lost or destroyed. Some we can't read. Others aren't true. Or they are biased. Or they don't tell us enough.

There are, for instance, the written records of the Etruscans, the mysterious people who lived in the middle of Italy in early Roman days. Being much less civilized, the Romans took over a great deal from these older inhabitants of Italy, whose skills they greatly admired. Noble Roman youths even used to be sent to the Etruscan town of Caere to pick up culture and polish. They would come back to Rome speaking Etruscan—the way we speak French. All the same, the Romans envied the Etruscans and fought them bitterly and at last succeeded in destroying their cities. Though it was impossible to kill off every single Etruscan, the Romans managed to wipe them out as a nation and a people. The Etruscans disappeared from the map. And their language died.

Now they had a writing. It looks as if it might be easy to read because the letters are much like the Greek. Scholars can, in fact, read Etruscan. But they don't understand what they read. They know how to pronounce the words and know the meaning of about a hundred of them, but the rest is a mystery. Whole lifetimes have been spent trying to solve the riddle. Yet the scholars can't get anywhere with it—the hundred or so known words aren't enough to go on. If we could discover something written in both Etruscan and a language that is known, the key might be found. But none has turned up so far.

In the main, the Etruscan writings are short inscriptions on tombs, and almost always they repeat the same words. The longer Etruscan texts were, unhappily, all written on rolls of cloth. So they have turned to dust, for it is more than 2,000 years since the people vanished. There is just one exception. By a curious chance one inscribed roll of cloth is left to us. It was cut into strips and used to wrap round the mummy of an Egyptian lady in Alexandria. The embalming fluids preserved it. Scholars have spent years trying to decipher the 1,500 words of this text, but they can't even agree on what it's about. Some say it concerns funeral ceremonies. Some say it is a curse. Others suggest prayers to the gods. Others think that it is about statues struck by lightning.

You can well imagine that the Romans, who secretly looked up to the Etruscans so much, wrote about them in their own Latin tongue. But practically all those writings have been lost too. So we have almost nothing to tell us about this gifted people except the things they left behind them. Luckily they have left a great deal. For though the living cities of the Etruscans are gone, the cities of their dead remain. We have cemeteries used by the Etruscans for 800 years. One city of the dead alone covers 140 acres.

What are these tombs like and what do they have to tell us?

Most of them are cut out of the living rock and are just like houses only that they are underground. All that shows above is the upper part of the tomb, heaped over with soil and overgrown with grass. Today these houses of the dead are empty. For first the Romans and then other thieves helped themselves to the things the Etruscans put in their graves. But some of the tombs have paintings on the walls, and these pictures speak to us though the writings cannot. They show us how the Etruscans looked and dressed, how they feasted and danced, what musical instruments they had, what games and amusements they enjoyed, how they fished and hunted. We capture the wonderfully joyous spirit of that lost people.

Wall paintings reveal the joyous spirit of the Etruscans.

Some of the tombs have walls decorated with stucco reliefs. One famous one must have belonged to a military man, for the decorations are plaster copies of the armor and the weapons a fighting man would use. On one pillar are a huntsman's bag, the rudder of a boat, and a goose to do honor to the dead man's fowling skill. His wife, who shared the tomb with him, must have been a noted housewife in her day to judge from the decorations on the other side of the chamber. For here are plaster models of an egg whisk, a cheese, a duck, a pan for cooking, a jug, and other kitchen things. There is even a pussycat to complete the homelike picture.

But what of the objects themselves?

A single find tells us what kinds of things the robbers carried off.

In the year 1836 General Galassi and Archpriest Regolini of Cerveteri opened a large mound that stood in a vineyard at some distance from the Etruscan cemetery. After many attempts they found the doorway. Then by the light of their torches they made their way along a 60-foot passage and entered the house of the dead. No footstep had sounded on its stone floor for 3,000 years.

On a bronze bed lay the remains of a warrior with his bronze armor sunk on his dust. The king himself—for such he must have been, judging from the richness of the gifts—had not endured, but the things he had used and loved were all about him. Beside the bed stood a table with a censer, a shield, and arrows. On the walls were more shields of bronze. The remains of his bronze-covered two-wheeled chariot lay by the door and his bronze-covered high-backed throne stood near.

The general and priest passed through to the inner chamber, but even now they were unprepared for the sight that greeted them. A mass of beautiful, frail, pale-gold jewelry lay on a stone bed and spilled over onto the floor. The body of the woman whom the jewels had decked had turned to dust. Earrings lay where the ears had been. Gold arm bands lay where the arms had been. A gold clasp had held her cloak together. Over the breast was a large round sheet of gold plate covered with a beautiful design of plants and animals. The lady had worn rings, necklaces, brooches, and pins of gold. Yet all this vast quantity was so lightly spun by the

Beautiful bronze statues of warriors and monsters

Etruscan goldsmiths that the whole weighed "hardly more than a heap of rose-petals."

Countless objects had been provided for the dead—magnificently worked bronze cauldrons were there, silver bowls, and great earthenware jars filled with grain, oil, honey, and eggs. Plates and jugs of silver stood about. The jewelry would have filled a shop. On two of the queen's small silver bowls were inscribed the words *Mi Larthia*—I am Larthia, or This is Larthia.

The words don't tell us much. But the things from the Galassi-Regolini tomb, which today fill an entire hall in the Vatican Museum, do.

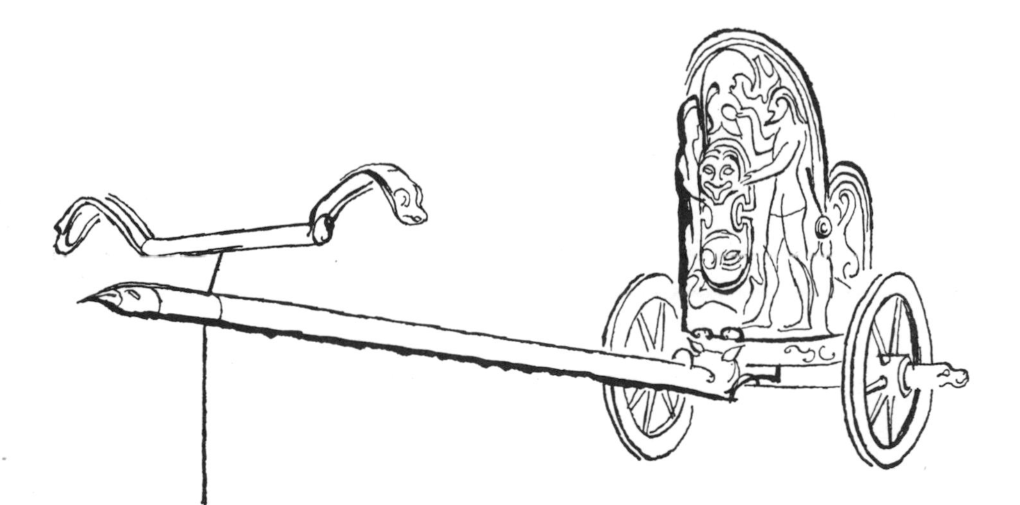

were discovered in Etruscan tombs, along with war chariots.

VII

On a Crest Above the Sea

What is true of the Etruscans, whose writings are a closed book to us, holds also for a people like the Saxons, whose records we can read and understand. For while the Saxons have left little in the way of writings, the things they have left behind them have much to say to us. In 1939 at Sutton Hoo a find was made that added a wonderfully vivid page to the story of those bold seamen who conquered Britain. It was the richest archaeological find ever made in England.

Sutton Hoo is on the coast of Suffolk. There, on the estate of Mrs. E. M. Pretty, on a crest a hundred feet above the sea, stood eleven ancient burial mounds. At high tide the sea came to within half a mile of them. Mrs. Pretty was curious about what was in the barrows and had three of them opened. But there was very little inside, for all three had been entered and robbed. Nevertheless, she decided to open a fourth mound. It was nine feet high and rather taller than the others.

The work had been going on only a short time when the explorers came upon rows of iron nails sticking into the firm-packed sand. They got the meaning at once. The nails were part of a ship—the wood had decayed but the nails were still in place. They knew that it had been a custom among the seafaring peoples living on the northeast coast of Europe to bury their important dead in ships. Archaeology had shown that kings, great nobles, and even great ladies had been buried so. This ship, then, whose nails they saw in even rows, was a burial ship. "It's not likely," they thought, "that we'll find untouched treasure below. Not after the experience of those other three mounds. But there's *something* important down there." They thought they had better get some help, so they asked the British Museum and the Office of Works for advice.

A team of experts was got together. The problem the experts set themselves seemed almost impossible: to get a complete impression of the ship although the ship itself no longer existed. But, using the most careful techniques of archaeology, they did it. In the end the whole shape of the ghost ship stood revealed in the sand. It was a great open rowing boat eighty feet long by fourteen broad. Thirty-eight rowers had driven it across the sea without the help of any sail. The steering was by a great broad-bladed oar over the stern. There was no true keel and there was no deck. The men who went raiding in that ship had had plenty of bailing to do in rough weather on the open sea. Yet in just such ships the Saxons had invaded Britain—and then gone back across the sea for their wives and children!

But long before these facts came clear, the buried treasure had been found. It was all there. Robbers had

The shape of a ghost ship stood revealed in the sand, with gold,

indeed tried to get it, but they had missed the burial chamber. The archaeologists came upon the hole the thieves had dug, and down on its bottom they found bones, the remains of a fire, and a piece of a jug. Evidently a meal had been eaten down there. The piece of

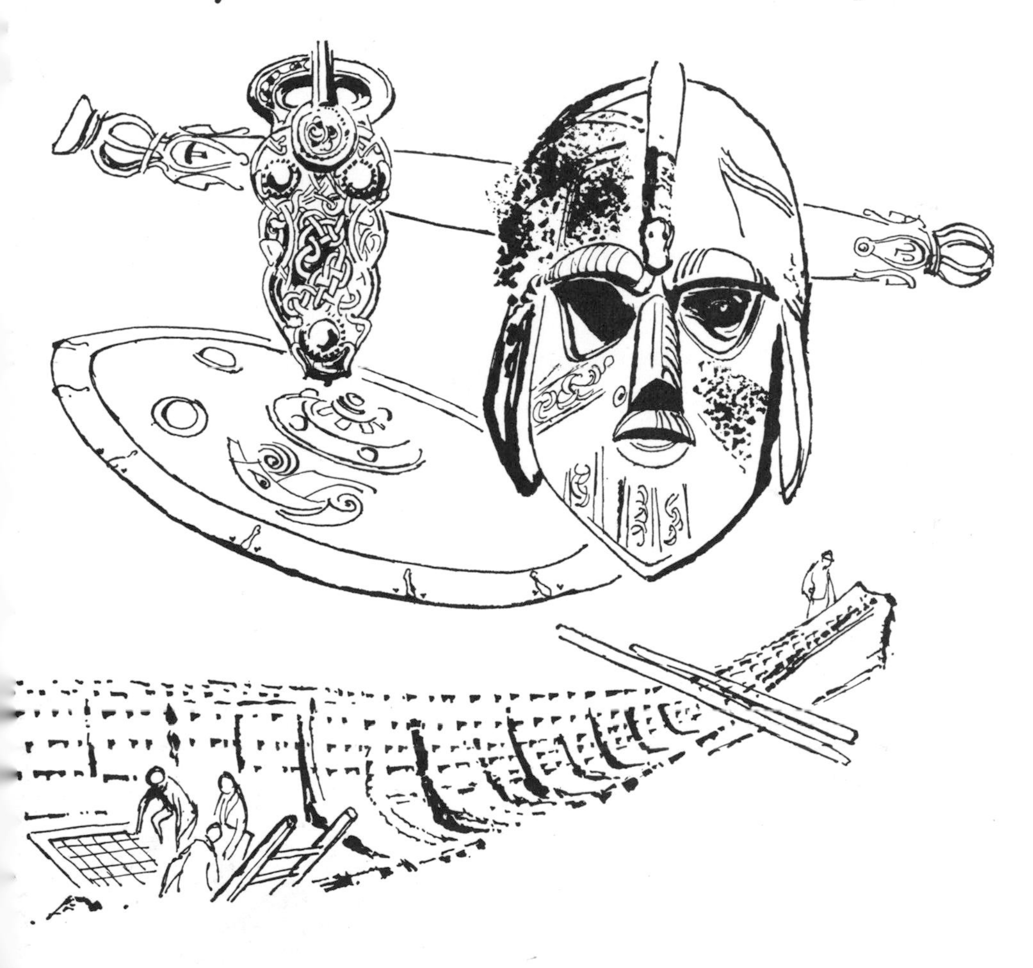

silver, and bronze treasure piled amidships.

jug revealed that the attempted robbery had taken place about 350 years earlier—in Shakespeare's day.

The treasure lay amidships. Walls and a gabled roof had once surrounded it, but, being made of wood, they had long ago turned to dust. Everything had been put directly on the ship's bottom in a confused pile. Gold jewelry mingled with silver plate, weapons and bowls, cups, and drinking horns, leather shoes, bone combs, gourd vessels with gilt-bronze rims, and the remains of an iron-bound bucket. Of a large shield only the iron boss was left—the wooden frame had rotted. Three long iron spears were thrust through one of the handles of a large bronze bowl. The remains of a small stringed instrument with wooden pegs lay in another. Eight silver bowls were nested together, and under them lay two silver spoons with the names *Saulos* and *Paulos* engraved in Greek. There was a great deal of rusted iron mail, an iron standard for a banner with a little bronze deer on top, and a ceremonial whetstone.

A handsome iron helmet was one of the great prizes of the hoard. Its crest was covered with silver, the bronze eyebrows were inlaid with silver wire, the mustache was bronze. A rusted sword with jeweled gold pommel and hilt lay among an amazing lot of gold objects. Under a purse lid of gold were forty gold coins.

For whom had all these things been buried?

The surprising thing was that there was no evidence that anyone had been buried in the ship. That could mean only one thing—the body had not been recovered. Either the royal person in whose name the ship and treasure had been buried was killed in battle or he was drowned. From the coins and other clues the experts were able to figure out that the burial had taken place between A.D. 650 and 670. But who the absent dead man was nobody could say for sure.

"Perhaps it was the Saxon King Aethelhere," someone suggested. "He was killed in a battle in 655. He had been baptized, to be sure—those silver spoons with *Saul* and *Paul* on them confirm it—but the baptism went only skin-deep. He would have loved a Pagan burial like this—with a barrow high on a crest and a clear view to the sea."

VIII

Heinrich Schliemann Finds Troy

How do archaeologists know where to dig?

The whole earth is archaeology's province, and archaeologists dig wherever there seems to be the chance of a find. Most often something showing above the ground invites them to explore. Once in a while the wearing away of a shore, a shifting wind, a sudden drought reveals the lost works of Man. Sometimes a farmer turning up the soil with his plow finds something that sets archaeologists digging. Sometimes clues come to them from folklore, legends, books.

The most famous of all archaeologists, the German Heinrich Schliemann, got his lead in this last strange way. His discovery rang round the world and wrote his name in golden letters in the book of archaeology. And all of it happened on account of his faith in a poem.

The story of that famous find goes back to the Christmas before Heinrich was eight years old, for it was then that his father gave him a copy of Jerrer's *Universal History*. There was in this book a picture of Homer's Troy in flames. Heinrich riveted his eyes on it. He studied every detail of the picture, which showed the huge walls of Troy with its Scaean Gate. Out of this gate a Trojan hero was escaping carrying his old father on his back and holding his young son by the hand. Heinrich knew all about Troy. His education had begun with the *Iliad*, Homer's poem about the ten years' war which the Achaeans had fought against Troy and won at last only through the stratagem of the Wooden Horse.

"Father," the boy said at last, "did Troy really have such huge walls as the picture shows?"

"It did."

"Then," said Heinrich, "they can't possibly have been completely destroyed. Vast ruins of them must still remain." And then and there he made up his mind that someday he would dig up Troy from beneath the dust of ages.

Now, not only had the famous city disappeared—

even its story had for most people become just a myth. Of the millions who read and loved the *Iliad*, nearly all had come to doubt that any part of the wonderful tale of Troy was true—in spite of the fact that the poet made it all sound so real.

And the reason was this: The *things* Homer described in his poem were far and away beyond anything the crude Greeks of his own day possessed. The whole civilization he pictured was on a higher level than his own. Was it possible that Greece had gone backward?

"No," people said, "Homer invented everything. There never was such a person as Priam, King of Troy. His son Paris never carried off fair-haired Helen, Menelaus' wife. The Trojan War was never fought to bring her back. And more than likely there never was a Troy at all. The whole thing is just the poet's fancy."

Heinrich Schliemann had no such doubts. To him everything about Troy was real. Through all the hard struggle of his boyhood and youth he clung to the dream of digging up the lost city. And when at forty-six he found himself a rich man, the time had come, he decided, to turn the dream into reality.

But where was the most likely place to dig?

The few people who believed there really was a Troy

said the city had stood on a certain little hill on the coast of Asia Minor. Schliemann went over to see.

"Impossible," he said after the very first glance. "It is three hours from here to the coast. That doesn't fit in with the facts of Homer's story at all. Moreover, how could the huge palace of Priam with its sixty-two rooms, together with all the other buildings and the Great Scaean Gate have stood on such a little hill?"

He began to look around for a more likely spot. When his eyes fell on a hill called Hissarlik, he knew he had found it. It was only an hour from the coast and, besides, the hill looked like such a wonderful natural fortification. Schliemann got permission from the Turkish government, hired a hundred laborers or so, and in April of 1870 began to dig.

It wasn't long before he realized that many other people besides himself had thought Hissarlik a wonderful natural fortification. A few feet below the top he came upon the ruins of a city. Under it lay other ruins. Under them were others still—how many he couldn't yet tell. For the lower he dug, the more ruins he found, ruins always standing on top of other ruins. He had thought to dig up Troy. He was digging up much more. City after city had stood upon this spot which looked so easy to defend—and was not. City after city had fallen to the enemy. Always new people had come and settled on top. They had filled in the shattered lower floors and the streets choked with rubbish; they had leveled the ground and built once more.

Now it is exciting to find anything out of the distant past—be it an arrowhead, a clay pot, or a pin. To find a forgotten city is far more exciting. To find seven cities one under another—and later several more would be found as archaeologists dug into other points on the hill—was an event that thrilled the whole civilized world. And yet it wasn't the number of cities Schliemann found that stirred the folk who read the news. It was the thought that one of the seven was Homer's Troy. Troy, that city of glorious adventure which they had come—oh, so reluctantly—to believe was fancy, was actually fact. Schliemann had found Troy!

But which of the seven cities was Homer's Troy?

It was clear enough that the ruins at the top were those of Roman Ilium. It was just as clear that the rude things at the bottom belonged to a people of the Stone Age. But in between?

The record wasn't easy to read and, as a matter of fact, Schliemann read it wrong. He decided that the

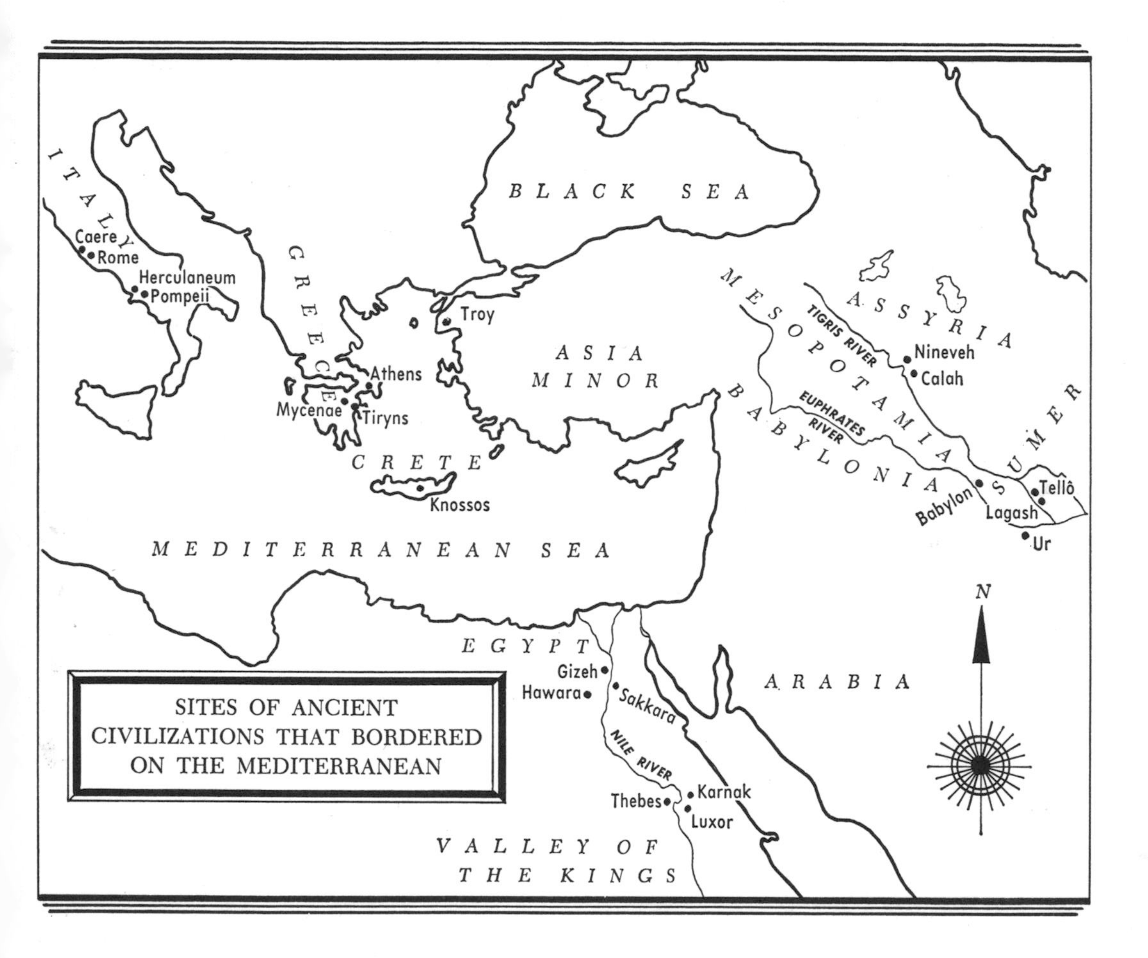

second city from the bottom was Homer's Troy. Here he had found thick walls and a gate and the ruins of a house filled with remarkable things. He called the house "Priam's Palace." The gate, he was certain, was the Scaean Gate. Not till three years after he died were his conclusions set aside in favor of ruins much nearer the top, a city the archaeologists called VIIa. This had really been Homer's Troy, but Schliemann had missed it, for at the point where he was digging, it had been completely leveled by the Romans.

The archaeologist had now been digging over three years. He had discovered—so he thought—the city of his dreams and had a whole museumful of wonderful things besides. But still, at bottom he was disappointed. He hadn't found any gold. And because he had been a desperately poor boy, gold had always been an important part of his dream. He was preparing to leave, for he had other plans in mind. He fixed the fifteenth of June, 1873, as the last day.

And on the fourteenth he found the gold!

It was early morning. He was standing with his young Greek wife twenty-eight feet down in the diggings. Suddenly a copper object imbedded in the wall of the pit caught his eye. From behind it came the distinct gleam of gold.

"Go at once!" he said breathlessly to his wife. "Tell the men to go home. Say it is my birthday and that I have just remembered it. Tell them everyone will get paid just the same."

Handful by handful Schliemann lifted out the golden objects.

The thought in his mind was—thieves. If he didn't send the diggers away, everything would be stolen.

Feverishly he cut around the copper object. He put his hand in—and closed his fingers on golden treasures. His wife by this time had returned. She spread out her shawl, and handful by handful Schliemann lifted out and laid the golden objects on it. They were dazzling. They were beyond price.

But this was not the place to examine the find. Not till Schliemann and his wife were safe in their own room did they sort and count the treasure. There were two gold diadems—one made up of 90 chains—and 12,271 rings. There were twenty-four gold necklaces. Besides these there was a bewildering pile of small things—heart-shaped plaques for sewing on garments, eardrops, buttons, and so on.

Schliemann's hands trembled as he hung the golden chains around his wife's neck and held the rings to her ears. "These are the treasures of Priam," he thought. He placed the diadem on her brow, wondering if perhaps Helen herself had worn it.

It was the high point of his career, he felt, the high point of his life. Would he ever again find anything that would have such meaning for him?

IX

Golden Mycenae

What Schliemann wanted to do was cross over to Greece and dig up the grave of King Agamemnon. This famous king had been general-in-chief over all the Achaean princes who warred on Troy. Also he had ruled over "golden" Mycenae. That word *golden* had a great deal of appeal for Schliemann. Not that he wanted to keep any of the treasure he found for himself—he just got a thrill out of finding gold.

Unlike Troy, Mycenae had not vanished entirely from the face of the earth. The broken city walls—in some places fifty feet high—still stood on the main

hill. Beside them rose a gate carved with lions. And on the surrounding slopes were tombs shaped like beehives. The archaeologists said that somewhere out there on those slopes the grave of Agamemnon lay—if it lay anywhere.

But Schliemann didn't agree with them. He had an old Greek guidebook which said Agamemnon's grave lay *in*side the walls. So inside the walls he ordered a pit to be dug. And to everybody's amazement, twenty-three feet down he came upon five graves hewn out of the solid rock.

Schliemann had thought "Priam's Treasure" a matchless find. But compared with the hoard he now drew from the graves it was a trifle. Golden masks and breastplates, golden armbands and girdles, golden disks and leaves decked the fifteen bodies in the graves. The women were simply loaded with gold and jewels—rings, bracelets, necklaces, diadems, pendants, leaves, butterflies, flowers. One of the skeletons had a crown on its head.

Schliemann was nearly beside himself as day after day his wife carried home a basket full of gold. "All the museums in the world put together do not possess one-fifth of the trinkets and jewels I have found," he announced. But what gave him the greatest joy was that he had found Agamemnon. He didn't doubt it for a minute. He was overcome with awe as he raised to his lips the golden mask which he believed had covered the face of the famous king. Life couldn't hold a greater thrill, he felt.

The graves were not really those of Agamemnon and his kin. They belonged to an earlier time. But so far as archaeology was concerned, it didn't matter.

Archaeologists began to dig all over the country to find other lost cities. But only Schliemann seemed to have luck. He started digging on a site where some burnt walls showed above ground. Everybody else thought those walls belonged to a very much later time, but he was convinced they were part of the ancient fortress of Tiryns. And, sure enough, they were. The very first summer his workmen laid bare the floor plan of an ancient palace.

It was easy to see from the decorations that Tiryns had been rich and beautiful. And the huge walls around the palace confirmed it. They showed by their very size that there had been something here vastly worth protecting. In some parts they were fifty-seven feet thick and had rooms and galleries built right in them.

Here was another proof that a wonderfully civilized people had lived along Greece's eastern shore earlier then anyone had imagined.

But now archaeology was going to show something even more surprising.

A Tiryns wall painting of a huntsman holding a hound.

X

In the Palace of Minos

Around the year 1900 there arrived in Crete—which is the big island south of Greece—an Englishman by the name of Arthur Evans. Keeper of the Ashmolean Museum at Oxford, he had come to hunt for some more examples of a mysterious kind of writing. In Athens he had picked up some little seal stones with this unknown kind of writing on them. He thought it might be Cretan. And the reason he thought so was that legend said Crete had once been a great and powerful land.

A mighty king called Minos had ruled over Crete, so legend said. His power had stretched far beyond his capital at Knossos, for his navy ruled the seas. It was for him that the architect Daedalus built the Labyrinth. This was a vast structure made to be lost in—a maze. Here, according to the legend, Minos kept his man-eating monster Minotaur, half man, half bull. Every nine years seven Athenian maidens and seven youths were sent as tribute to King Minos, to be served up to the Minotaur. And this had gone on till the hero Theseus, son of the Athenian king, had battled with the Minotaur in the dim depths of the Labyrinth and slain him.

Now in his wanderings over Crete, Arthur Evans came to a certain hill on which stood great blocks of gypsum that were part of a ruin. They had on them some of the writing he was hunting for. But as he stood looking at the blocks, a very different project took hold of his mind. Evans was seized with a wild desire to dig. For this spot was supposed to be the site of Knossos, Minos' capital. "Perhaps," he thought excitedly, "I can dig up the palace of King Minos. Who knows? I might dig up the Labyrinth itself!"

He bought the hill and began to dig. And almost at once things happened. Walls appeared, then more and more. In two months' time two acres of a vast building lay before him. A year passed, two years. A time came when Evans could look over six acres of ground and see the ruins stretching over all. He stayed on the job a quarter of a century.

He dug and dug. The palace, which had been several stories high, was built around a great court. There were so many rooms and the plan was so confusing that Evans wondered how the people found their way around. The king's wealth had come from olive oil, and here were the rooms where the palace had pressed it. Here, again, were the storerooms with many of the oil jars still in place. And here were the rooms where the jars had been made. Rooms, rooms, rooms. Rooms where metal work had been done. Rooms where pots had been painted. Rooms for worship. Rooms for sleep. Rooms, rooms, rooms. Corridors, staircases, courts.

"It is like a maze," Evans thought. "Can this be the Labyrinth?"

Not only the confusing plan made Evans think so. In a thousand places on the walls and elsewhere he saw a mark like this:

He knew it was the *Labrys* or Double-Ax, the mysterious sign of the Mother Goddess of Crete. "Doubtless

The reconstructed south palace steps at Knossos.

this *Labrys* gave the Labyrinth its name," he thought. "The Labyrinth was really this palace of Minos."

He fell in love with the queen's apartments, gay with paintings of dolphins playing in the sea and girls dancing. Everything in her rooms had been made for joy and comfort. There was even a terra-cotta bathtub for the queen. But this didn't surprise Evans. For all over the palace he saw devices that many houses in some parts of the world don't have today. There were drains and ventilators and lavatories, shafts for light and sinks and pits for trash. Anybody could see that a very modern sort of people had lived here.

One of the great moments was when Evans dug out the throne room and looked on the high-backed stone throne that still stood in its place against the wall. He knew he was looking at the oldest throne in all the world. The stone benches on which the counselors had sat still ran around three sides of the chamber. "It must have been a beautiful room," he thought as he picked up bits of gold foil and crystal and green faïence and lapis lazuli from the floor. He had a skilled artist restore the paintings that had decorated the walls. Two brilliantly colored griffins had guarded the throne, one on either side of it.

On the floor of the throne room he found an overturned oil jar and some broken sacred vessels. "What do they mean?" Evans thought. He looked through an opening in the wall that led to an inner chamber. There stood a shrine of the Great Mother Goddess of Crete. "This was their Holy of Holies," Evans thought. "Was the Priest-King performing some sacred ceremony when the Destroyers came? Is that the meaning of the overturned jar and the broken vessels? Was he rudely interrupted?"

There was so much he didn't know. Perhaps he would never know it until the Minoan writing was deciphered. Would it ever be? He had found thousands of tablets inscribed with the curious signs. But he couldn't read any of them.

He could not know that in 1954 Michael Ventris, an English architect, would discover the key to one type of Minoan writing.

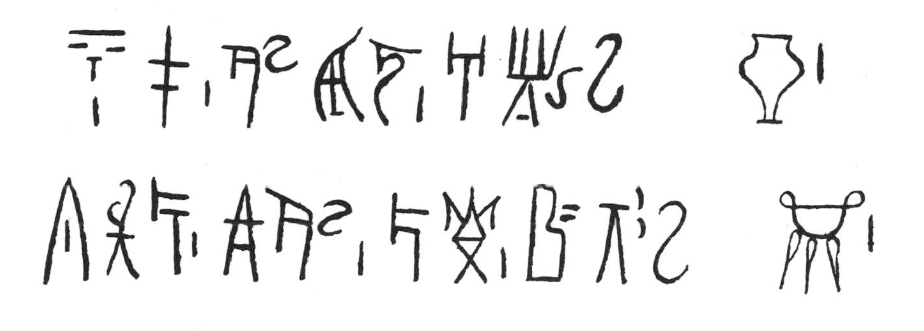

XI

The Minoans

Evans was terribly curious about the people who had lived in the Labyrinth. He had called them the *Minoans*. But what had the Minoans looked like? To what race had they belonged?

One day the explorer came face to face with one of them. He was a cupbearer painted on a wall.

The man looked like no human being Evans had ever seen. He was quite dark, with full lips and curly black hair done up in a crest. But he was not a Negro. He looked like a European. The profile of his face, except for the lips, was like that of an ancient Greek. He was small, clean-shaven, athletic-looking, with a slender

Five Minoan ladies with flounced skirts and puffed sleeves.

waist. He was dressed in a figured loincloth, and the upper part of his body was bare.

Later, as Evans came on painting after painting, he got well acquainted with the Minoans. The ladies astonished him. They seemed so modern. They wore clothes that looked like the latest models from Paris—fancy flounced skirts and jackets with puffed sleeves. Sometimes they wore gloves. Or they left them hanging from their folding chairs as they sat in the front seats watching the shows. They looked gay, lively, and very up-to-date. With a row of kiss curls across their foreheads, they didn't look at all like women who had lived 3,300 years ago. They didn't seem to go with the men in the patterned loincloths at all.

But Minos himself?

Many times Evans tried to imagine the last mighty ruler of Crete. What had he looked like—this great king who had made such an impression on the people of his own time that the legends were full of him?

The king didn't appear in any of the group pictures. But one day Evans came on him alone. He was so different from what the explorer had imagined that Evans was taken aback. Minos was young and graceful. There was nothing of awe or terror about him. He walked lightly through a meadow gay with lilies and reeds. He was strong, majestic. On his bare chest he wore a necklace of fleurs-de-lis. On his head was a crown of the same flowers, topped with three magnificent peacock's feathers.

Where was the king going? What was he about to do? There was an air of something sacred about the picture—the lilies were sacred flowers. Was he about to perform a religious ceremony? His right hand was on his chest, but his left was stretched down. Had there been more to the picture? Was he perhaps leading along a sacred animal, one of those griffins that gods and priests were often pictured leading?

Evans knew he was looking on the last of the dark-skinned kings of Crete. Those powerful kings had ruled the sea. They had been so sure of their dominion, had felt so safe in their island realm, that they had built no walls at Knossos. The navy had protected the capital. For 600 years the navy had enabled Knossos to be the star and center of a wonderful life. Yet the mighty navy had been overcome at last. Around the year 1400 B.C. Knossos had fallen.

"Who were the destroyers?" Evans wondered. "Were they the same people who laid waste Mycenae and broke down the giant walls of Tiryns?"

The story was shadowy, confused. Scholars would surely argue about it for years to come. But the important thing was the builders, not the destroyers. The important thing was all this light that Schliemann and Evans had shed on a thousand years of darkness. The magic spades of archaeology had dug up a lost people and their glamorous lost world!

XII

A Lost Key Is Found

We said that most things are very perishable. We said that usually all an archaeologist has to build his case on is scraps of stone and bone, pottery, glass, and metal. But in Egypt this isn't true. In Egypt things made of wood, leather, hair, linen, grass, and other materials that were once alive don't turn to dust in a few centuries. The dry desert soil keeps things forever.

Of course, this makes Egypt a paradise to dig in. But climate is only part of it. The other part is ancient Egyptian religion. Never has there been a people who buried so much to take into the next world with them. Out of Egyptian tombs archaeologists have dug up a whole world. We know more about the ancient Egyptians than we know about many people who lived much nearer our time.

Now the story of digging in Egypt is a very special one. Nobody needed to put spade to earth to prove that thousands of years ago Egypt had had a great civilization. The signs of it were all around. There were the pyramids. There were the giant statues. There were the obelisks and temples. They seemed to say: "Behold the might that once was Egypt!"

And yet that wonderful story was lost. It was lost because the key had been mislaid. Most of the foreigners who came to Egypt to gape at the pyramids didn't know what kings had built the stupendous tombs, or how they did it, or why. The visitors who scratched their names on the legs of the giant statues didn't know whose likeness they marred. They didn't know because these tombs and statues had all been built so long ago; now no one remembered the history of these objects and no one could read Egyptian writing any more. There the hieroglyphics were—circles, squares, triangles, half

moons, knots, loops. But what did they mean? Snakes, geese, owls, heads, lions, beetles, palm leaves, lotus flowers, people squatting, people holding up their hands, people walking—nobody could make any sense of them.

Then just by chance the mislaid key was found.

One of Napoleon's soldiers was digging a trench when his spade struck something hard. He dug all around the object and pulled it out. It was a flat stone about as big as a newspaper opened wide. There was writing on it. The soldier could see that some of it was the same queer kind that was on the obelisks and in the tombs.

He had no idea that he was looking at one of the greatest treasures ever found by man. For on this Rosetta Stone, as it came to be called, was a law written in three different writings. One was Greek, one was hieroglyphic, and one was the ancient Egyptian script used in business. Scholars jumped to the task. This kind of clue was just what they had been waiting for. They would compare the unknown writing with the known and work out the signs that way.

But working out the puzzle was much harder than any of them expected, and one by one they gave up in despair. Only the French scholar Champollion held on.

The soldier could see some queer kind of writing on the stone.

After twenty-three years he had one hundred and eleven of the signs worked out. There were thousands more, of course, but he was over the hump. The rest was just a question of time.

Meanwhile excited people were pouring into Egypt. There had been so much talk about hieroglyphs that every museum wanted to own some. Many private collectors did too. The way they fought to get their hands on Egyptian scrolls, you would have thought hieroglyphics were gold. Egypt was a madhouse. The idea seemed to be to get something quick before somebody else did. Get it and sell it to a museum. If the easiest way to reach a mummy was to batter a hole in a tomb with a battering ram, why, that was all right too.

While all this was going on, a little boy by the name of William Flinders-Petrie was growing up in England. Someday he would teach them the right way to dig. He was only dreaming about digging now. And yet already he knew more about it than the greedy looters who were turning Egypt upside down.

"*The earth ought to be pared away inch by inch to see all that is in it and how it lies,*" he said when he was only eight years old.

XIII

Battle of Wits

As a boy Petrie had had a passion for exactness. He was always thinking up devices for weighing and measuring things. And when in 1880 as a young man he went to Egypt, it was with the intent of measuring the Great Pyramid of Gizeh. His chief reason for doing this was to investigate a certain crackpot theory about the meaning of the measurements. He was equally curious, however, to find out if the ancient Egyptians had in fact been such matchless builders as they were said to be.

Petrie was to spend a good part of his life crawling in and out of tombs, but he hadn't been at it very long before he saw that the pyramid builders fully deserved their reputation. They had unbelievable daring. They used tremendous blocks of stone, such as no architect would dare to use today. Yet the Egyptians did it all the time—without machinery.

Travelers used to stand gaping at the pyramids and ask, "How did they do it? Did they have secrets of building that have been lost?"

We don't have to ask that any more. Archaeology has shown us they had nothing of the kind.

In a certain tomb that goes back to 2000 B.C.—just about when the palace at Knossos was built—explorers found a drawing. It shows the Egyptians moving one of those gigantic statues they were so fond of setting around—statues weighing *hundreds of tons*. And there is no machine in sight. The statue is set on a sledge. A gang of 172 men is dragging the sledge along the sand.

All the Egyptian tricks of the trade were as simple as that. Suppose they wanted to quarry an obelisk—one of those tall, pointed stones weighing hundreds of tons that they set up in front of their temples. They would cut a groove in the rock where they wanted it split. Next they would drill holes along the groove. Then they would beat wooden pegs very tightly into the holes and pour on water. The wood swelled and the rock cracked along the groove. That's all there was to it. An obelisk only half cut out of the rock tells us the story.

Petrie had nothing but praise for the builders. Measuring the Great Pyramid around the base, he found it almost half a mile around; yet the sides were so even that he could put his thumb on the amount of error. "Laying out the base of the Great Pyramid was a triumph of skill," he pronounced. His voice had awe in it when he talked about the huge blocks of stone in one of the chambers inside the Pyramid. The Egyptians had used nine-foot jeweled copper saws to cut the blocks. They had cut them so exactly that the mortar holding them together was no thicker than a sheet of paper! "Such patience and skill have gone out of the world," he declared.

"But what an awful waste!" you might think. "All that work just for a tomb!"

It didn't seem like waste to King Khufu. He was perfectly willing to keep a hundred thousand men working thirty years to build the Great Pyramid. His palace would last him his lifetime. But his tomb would be his home forever. He had to make sure that his precious mummy and the treasures buried with it would be safe.

To understand how the King's mind worked, you have to know about the Ka. The Ka was the dead Egyptian's spirit or double. The tomb was a house for the Ka. It spent much of its time in the tomb. It did there all the things the dead man had done when he was alive. It ate there and drank and enjoyed itself in the tomb. *But it could do these things only as long as the body was safe*. If anything happened to the body, that was the end of the Ka.

You see now why the Egyptians learned to preserve dead bodies by using aromatic oils. Also you can better understand why they buried so much to take into the next world with them. The Ka needed everything the living person had used—his clothes and his jewels, his furniture, his dishes, food of all kinds, books, games, and so on.

Now all these wonderful things—and you may be sure that everything belonging to a king was very wonderful—were a strong temptation to robbers. "I'll build my tomb so big," Khufu decided, "that robbers will get discouraged when they just look at it. They won't even *try* to get in and steal my belongings and destroy my mummy as they have those of my ancestors."

The robbers got in just the same. They found the

secret entrance on the north side of the pyramid in the third tier of stones. They explored the passages, corridors, halls, and rooms. They stole everything. They destroyed the mummy to make sure the king's Ka would do them no harm. They left nothing except the granite sarcophagus in which the coffin had lain.

And the same thing happened to all the pyramids of Gizeh. Size had been a mistake. Just because the tombs were so big they had tempted robbers. "Wonderful things inside!" the pyramids had seemed to say.

What was to be done? It was plain that size was not the answer. How protect the mummy and the treasure?

When Petrie was exploring the brick pyramid of Amenemhat III at Hawara, he found out what the kings of Egypt tried next. They pitted their wits against the robbers and decided to build smaller pyramids but to build them so cleverly that the robbers would be balked.

They weren't. Petrie found King Amenemhat's sarcophagus rifled and empty.

It had taken the archaeologist months to get to the tomb chamber. For he couldn't find the entrance to the pyramid and had had to mine his way in. When at last the plan of the tomb was clear to him, it was so fantastic that he could hardly believe it. And he couldn't help admiring the robbers. How persistent those fellows had been!

They had found the entrance Petrie himself couldn't find. It was in an unusual place—on the south side of the pyramid. But that was only the first small step to their goal. A long staircase took them down through pitch darkness into a room out of which there seemed to be no exit. In vain they went over the walls and floor. At last they had found the trap door. It was in the roof! They had broken through this—only to find themselves facing a passage chock-full of blocks of stone.

That didn't stop them. Step by step they had mined their way through the stone. And when they were through, they found themselves up against a dead wall. The passage was a blind. The architect had put it there just to take their attention off the real passage, which all the while had been standing wide open.

Dashing down the real passage, the robbers entered a second empty chamber. But they knew what to look for now. They found the trap door and slid it aside. Another passage was before them. It led to another chamber whose secret exit they had to find.

Clambering out once more, the robbers had found

themselves in yet another passage. It led to still another chamber. And here two wells opened up in the floor. They looked as if they led to the tomb chamber. But the robbers had not been fooled. They understood that these were false wells. They guessed that the architect had put them there to throw them off the scent.

The chamber itself, however, was a problem. It was nearly filled with stone. The robbers had pulled all this stone down, hoping to find an exit, but there was no exit. They hunted along the passage floor. They found a filled-in cross-trench. They followed it right up to the tomb chamber, and here the worst difficulty of all faced them. The tomb chamber had no door. The only way in was through the roof. To get in they would have to raise up one of the immense roof blocks. And it weighed forty-five tons! It was beyond them. They couldn't lift a weight like that.

But they had not given up. The robbers had bored a hole in the hard sandstone roofing block. And they had got in.

XIV

Tut-ankh-Amen

The kings were at their wits' end. There seemed to be no way of stopping the robbers. What next?

Now the Egyptian kings might easily have saved their precious mummies if they had been willing to do what people of the middle class did. Those people were satisfied to take with them into the next world little models of the things they had used and loved. Robbers weren't interested in models of wood and clay. Only future archaeologists would make a fuss about them. But the kings refused to make such a sacrifice. They wouldn't compromise. They wanted the real things, not make-believe.

A model boat and crew found in an Egyptian tomb.

So at last they decided on a desperate plan. They would *hide* their tombs from the eyes of man.

"But why was this *desperate?*" you might wonder.

The reason was this. Beside each royal tomb there stood a little temple. It was a very important part of the tomb because to this little temple the dead man's friends and relatives brought their presents. Here food was left for the king's Ka. So the temple couldn't be hidden along with the tomb. It had to be out in plain sight, located in a convenient place for the king's friends to get to—his friends and his priests and all the various people who were paid to deliver food and drink for the king's Ka. This meant that the temple would have to be separated from the tomb. And that wasn't going to be pleasant for the Ka. Every day it would have to travel from the tomb to the temple and back again.

That's why hiding the tomb was a desperate plan. But it was the only possible plan. And it was carried out. The king's tomb temple was set up in the City of the Dead, just across the river from Thebes, the capital. And the king's mummy and all his treasures were buried secretly in a tomb hidden from the eyes of man. The place chosen was a barren little valley to the north of the cemetery.

It was about 1500 B.C. when a desperate Egyptian king started this new plan. After that for 500 years every king did the same thing—each was buried in the same little valley. It came to be called the Valley of the Tombs of the Kings.

And did that solve the robber problem?

You can guess. So long as powerful kings sat on the throne, the dead kings had some peace. But when the kings of Egypt became weaklings, tomb robbery grew into a regular business. And those who were supposed to protect the cemetery from robbers were the very biggest robbers of all. Was it any wonder? For 500 years the fabulous wealth of the kings of Egypt had been buried in one tiny valley. The dearest treasures of thirty kings lay there. Any risk was worth-while, robbers thought, to get their hands on some of that treasure.

So, naturally, when archaeologists began to dig in the Valley of the Tombs of the Kings, they didn't have much luck. They met with disappointment after disappointment. Always the robbers had been there before them. Once only did an explorer come upon a tomb that had been only partly rifled. It wasn't a royal tomb—just one belonging to a member of the grand nobility—yet it showed as never before how grand and rich the funeral things were. Every archaeologist in Egypt was thrilled. What would they not have given to see one single royal tomb just as it was when the king was buried! It was the dream of every explorer to find one.

Dreams cost nothing. After that find everybody's hopes went up. But very little happened, and the time came when nearly everybody thought there was no use digging in the Valley any more. "There is nothing left there," people said.

There were two men, however, who had not lost hope. They didn't believe they could find an untouched royal tomb. That seemed a wild dream now. Yet they did believe the Valley still held some secrets.

The two men were Lord Carnarvon and Howard Carter. Lord Carnarvon was not an archaeologist. He was an English gentleman interested in the arts who had gone to Egypt on account of his health. He had become interested in digging, but as he knew nothing about it, he had asked Howard Carter to help him. The two men had become instant friends and had worked as a team for sixteen years. Carter had been trained by Petrie himself.

Now they weren't planning to dig blindly. They were on the lookout for a particular tomb, the tomb of the boy king Tut-ankh-Amen who had ruled about fifty years after Knossos fell.

To most people this seemed silly. "The tomb of Tut-ankh-Amen has already been found!" they said. They were referring to a pit in which some things had been discovered with the names of Tut-ankh-Amen and his queen on them. But Carnarvon and Carter didn't believe the king had been buried in this pit. "It is too small for a royal burial," they said. "The things were put there later."

Not only did the two men believe that the tomb of Tut-ankh-Amen was still to be found. They thought they knew the best place to dig for it. This was the very center of the Valley. For right there two jars had been dug up containing bits of things that had been used at King Tut's funeral.

The site the explorers chose looked absolutely hopeless even to them. It was piled high with dirt thrown out by other diggers. But in the fall of 1917 they started work and in the next five years went over every inch of the ground. There was just one spot they didn't touch. This was a small piece of ground covered with the ruins of some stone huts. Once those huts had sheltered the workmen who had built the tomb of King Rameses VI.

In November, 1922, Howard Carter began digging in this area. And things happened so fast that they left him dazed. Under the very first hut the men attacked they found a shallow step. Soon the top edges of a stairway showed. Twelve steps led down—and at the level of the twelfth was the upper part of a sealed and plastered doorway.

Carter was wild with excitement. Anything might lie behind that door! But this was Carnarvon's discovery, too, and he was in England. So, to the astonishment of his diggers, Carter ordered them to fill in the stairway again. Then he sent a cable to Lord Carnarvon: "At last have made wonderful discovery in Valley. A magnificent tomb with seals intact. Recovered same for your arrival. Congratulations."

The story of what happened then has been told a thousand times. For never before had such a find been made. Tut-ankh-Amen's tomb was one of the great sensations of our century.

In two weeks' time Lord Carnarvon was on the spot. The stairway was uncovered. There was a worrisome patch in the upper part of the doorway, showing that someone had already broken through. Robbers had been here before them. They had been caught. But how much was left in the tomb?

The explorers broke down the door. Behind it was a passage filled with stone. When they had cleared it, they found themselves before a second sealed door. Carter made a tiny hole in it and passed a candle through.

"Can you see anything?" Carnarvon asked as Carter stood there dazed and astonished.

"Yes, wonderful things!"

What Carter saw has been pictured again and again. Newspapers, magazines, and books have shown the gilt couches, the inlaid caskets, the vases, shrines, beds, chairs, chariots, and the golden inlaid throne of Tut-ankh-Amen. There was no coffin in the room. But on one side stood two statues. They faced each other, and between them was a sealed doorway. "Behind it must be other rooms," Carter thought. "And in one of them, beyond a doubt, we will find the king himself."

It was many months before the explorers had done

their duty by that museumful of treasure. But at last everything was photographed, labeled and mended, and packed and shipped. They turned now to the door between the statues, breaking it down.

An immense shrine covered all over with gold was before them. It almost filled the room. Inside it, they knew, the king lay and they would see him in all his glory. But they didn't start work at once. They only made sure the seal of the shrine was unbroken. Then, unrolling the wire of their electric light, they passed to the farthest end of the chamber.

To their surprise, they were not up against a dead wall. A low door stood open before them. They passed through—and gasped. They were in a room that held things far more beautiful than anything they had seen before. And everything looked as fresh as if it had been put there yesterday. There wasn't a speck of dust. As they looked about them at the statues and shrines and caskets and chests, they could hardly believe these were things of 3,300 years ago. It seemed to them as if Tut-ankh-Amen had just died. It seemed to them as if they themselves were taking part in the King's funeral.

As it happened, Lord Carnarvon never lived to see Tut-ankh-Amen in all his glory. When the time came to dismantle the shrines, Carter had to work alone.

There were four of the shrines. They were nested one inside the other, and within the innermost lay a chest carved from a single block of yellow quartzite. Inside it, wrapped in folds of linen, was a beautiful coffin in the form of the boy king. A second coffin lay inside, and inside the second coffin was a third. It was strangely heavy. Carter could hardly believe it when this third coffin proved to be made of solid gold.

"What wonder the robbers always managed to find the royal tombs!" he thought. The gold of that coffin was worth two and a half million dollars.

The mummy itself was surrounded by treasures. Over the face was a portrait mask of beaten gold. Under the mask was a diadem. Necklaces circled the throat. Breast-plates of gold were on the chest. Over the feet were gold sandals, over the toes and fingers gold sheaths. About the arms were bracelets of gold and silver inlaid with precious stones. In all, 143 objects lay about the body.

What was the treasure worth? Carter didn't try to guess; he didn't really care. He knew that the tomb of Tut-ankh-Amen was priceless. Of all the royal tombs it alone had escaped—or almost escaped—the robbers. Yet it alone was enough to bring to life the glamor and glitter of the earth's mightiest builders.

XV

Scholars and Sumerians

After Tut-ankh-Amen everything that came from the earth seemed pale by comparison. "Nobody will ever dig up anything half as exciting as that again," people said. But they were mistaken. What Leonard Woolley dug up at Ur was a good second to King Tut.

Ur is an old, old city that once flourished in Mesopotamia, which is the land between the Tigris and Euphrates Rivers. Abraham, whose name is familiar from the Bible, came from Ur.

Now all the ancient cities of Mesopotamia had utterly disappeared from the face of the earth even as Troy had. They had become huge, shapeless mounds. After 2,000 years nobody knew any more what cities they had been

—or, indeed, that they had been cities at all. Two thousand years is a long time. People remembered names—Nineveh, Babylon. They knew that once a people called the Assyrians had been the terror of that part of the world. They knew that the Babylonians had dragged

Out of just one mound Layard removed thirteen pairs of

whole nations into captivity. But nobody had an idea of what the conquerors had looked like, how they had dressed, how they had lived. If an artist wanted to draw a picture of an Assyrian, he had to do it out of his imagination. A single museum case—three feet square—held all the world knew about Nineveh and Babylon.

Then in 1842 a Frenchman named Paul Emile Botta began to dig in one of the mounds. He dug up walls with sculptures on them and a wedge-shaped writing. He stared at the stones in wonder. Before him were people with hooked noses, big eyes with heavy eyelids, and curly beards. They were fighting with bows and arrows and spears. They were besieging cities, scaling towered walls, torturing prisoners, carrying away cap-

enormous winged stone lions and bulls with human heads.

tives and spoil. Botta had come upon a page of history that no one knew. He had dug up the palace of the Assyrian King Sargon at Dur-Sharrukin (Sargonburgh).

This was the first of many discoveries. Next the Englishman Austen Layard started to dig. Out of one mound he took thirteen pairs of enormous winged stone lions and bulls with human heads. They had decorated the palace of Ashurnasirpal at Calah. Out of another mound he dug the ruins of Sennacherib's palace. For this monstrous heap of brick and dust he was stirring was the long-lost Assyrian Nineveh. Sennacherib, the great king, had been scarcely more than a dread name before. Now he was history. Here were his deeds pictured in stone. Here were the very cylinders on which he had had his inhuman deeds inscribed. Here in his own words was how he had plundered, captured, tortured, burned.

In two rooms that had been built on to the palace at a later time, Layard made the most important find of all. It was a hoard of thousands of books—part of the library of King Ashurbanipal. Each book was a number of clay tablets inscribed with the same wedge-shaped writing that was on the cylinders and stones. Nearly all were copies of Babylonian books.

Now there is no better way to the *thoughts* of a people than the books they have written. So it was a lucky thing that the key to the cuneiform writing had already been found. It had been found in spite of the fact that the mystery of the wedges was much harder to solve than the mystery of Egyptian hieroglyphics. For there was nothing like a Rosetta Stone to help the scholars work out the wedges. Moreover, there was a special difficulty here. *The same sign often stood for three different syllables!* Thus

the sign

might stand for *li-ib*. Or it might stand for *da-an*. Or it might stand for *ka-al*.

"That's impossible," people said when they first heard about it. "How can anybody read a language in which the selfsame sign stands for three different things? Those long-haired fellows are having a joke with us."

"No such thing," the scholars protested. "There really *is* such a language, and we *can* read it."

"Try us out," one scholar suggested. "Give us a piece of writing we have never seen before. Let each of us work it out by himself. Then see if we have all read the same thing or not."

The Royal Asiatic Society agreed. A piece of writing that had never yet been translated was sent to four different scholars. And they all read it the same way!

There was such a writing. But how could it be? Why should the Babylonians have invented so peculiar a writing?

"They didn't invent it," the answer came. "The Babylonians *borrowed* their writing from an entirely different people who spoke an altogether different tongue. And they applied the signs to their own language. It is all very complicated, but that's how it happened."

"What next!" people scoffed. "Just because you can't explain why one sign stands for several sounds, you go and *invent* a people. Why aren't there any inscriptions in their language? Who were these other people anyhow?"

"They were the Sumerians," the scholars answered. (They had made up the name. For in some very old inscriptions the kings of that region had called themselves "King of Sumer and Akkad.")

"Look for the Sumerians in the southernmost part of Mesopotamia," the scholars told the archaeologists. "For that's where the oldest inscriptions are coming from."

Ernest de Sarzec took up the challenge without knowing he was doing it. He just wanted to dig as Botta and Layard had done. He had been told about the mounds of Tellô in the south and went there—not very hopefully—to look the field over. To his joy he found the ground strewn with pieces of pottery, inscribed bricks, and bits of sculpture. But what interested him most was a piece of a huge statue with an inscription on the shoulder. It lay at the foot of the principal mound.

"That statue rolled down here from the height," he reasoned. "If I dig up there, I may bring up more things belonging to the same civilization."

His thinking proved right. He had barely started to dig when he began to uncover a large building. Then came a carved monument of a king called Eannatum and many stone statues of a king named Gudea, who had ruled in a city called Lagash. Two terra-cotta cylinders belonging to King Gudea were the greatest prize. Each was inscribed with about 2,000 lines of cuneiform, and this, just as the scholars had foretold, turned out to be a language entirely different from Babylonian.

When De Sarzec's statues and objects were set out in the Louvre Museum in Paris, there was just such a to-do about them as when Botta's sculptures were shown. The statues were rude and clumsy and some of them had no heads. But what of that? They were the work of the Sumerians, a people who up to this time had been unknown, a people who had ruled in Babylonia for 1,500 years before the Babylonians became a power!

"How strange!" everybody exclaimed. People couldn't get over the way the scholars had foretold the Sumerians—just from cuneiform writing, just because the same wedges stood for several different sounds.

The spades of the archaeologists dug away. And they brought to light one of the most gifted people the world has ever seen. In addition to inventing the wedge-shaped writing—perhaps the oldest writing in the world—the Sumerians had given the world the keystone arch. People had always thought that the Babylonians had invented this. But no, the Sumerians had had it before them. It had also been thought that the Babylonians were the first to write down the laws which have so deeply affected our own. No, they had copied them from the Sumerians.

"Where did these geniuses come from?" people wanted to know.

Which brings us right up to Leonard Woolley and the things he found at Ur.

XVI

Royal Funeral, 2500 B.C.

In every Sumerian city archaeologists uncovered the ruins of a certain type of mysterious building. It was a big, solid piece of brickwork that seemed to have been a tower. They called it the Ziggurat. Now what exactly had it been for?

Leonard Woolley, who had gone to Ur as head of the British Museum and University of Pennsylvania Joint Expedition, moved thousands of tons of rubbish to find out what that city's Ziggurat had looked like. It was the best preserved of them all, and he gave the clearest answer to what it had been for. The best part of his theory was that it suggested where those geniuses the Sumerians had come from.

"The Ziggurat," said Woolley, "was simply a man-made mountain. It was a 'Hill of Heaven,' a 'Mountain of God,' a 'high place' for the Sumerians to worship their gods on."

When it comes to religion, people are stubborn. They want to keep on doing what they have always done, what their fathers and their grandfathers and their remotest ancestors did before them. To Woolley it was clear the Sumerians had come from some hilly country—perhaps India. Back home they had worshiped their gods in the "high places." When they emigrated to Mesopotamia and found themselves in a vast level plain, they were troubled. How could they worship their gods, who dwelt on the mountaintops? "We'll *build* mountains for our gods," they said. There was plenty of mud around. So they made tons and tons of bricks and piled them into holy hills.

The Sumerians had done their best to make their artificial hills look real. In the Ziggurat of Ur they had set three blocks of bricks one on top of another. Each block was smaller than the one below, and the sides slanted inward to give the mountain its pointed shape and lead the eye up and up. To make their man-made mountain look more real, the Sumerians had even

Sketch of the Ziggurat of Ur as reconstructed.

planted trees on the terraces. Staircases had gone to the top to take the place of the mountain paths they once had climbed. On the very top stood a little one-room shrine to the Moon god, for whose sake all the huge mass of brickwork had been built.

Woolley stayed twelve years on the job at Ur. From the ruins of that lost city he drew a world of strange things that brought the vanished Sumerians to life. But his most spectacular find was in the royal cemetery. Nothing like it had ever been found before. Nothing like it has been found since.

The royal tombs Woolley was digging up went back

Golden cups and bowls were placed in the royal tombs.

about 4,500 years. So he wasn't surprised to find human sacrifice had been part of every royal burial. Always in an undisturbed royal tomb he was sure to find two to four attendants who had been buried with the dead ruler. They were as much a part of the tomb furniture as the golden cups and bowls and other offerings. They were there to serve the king or queen in the next world.

The thing that did surprise Woolley was that the attendants in the tomb were not the *only* people sacrificed at the burial. In a pit *outside* the tomb as many as seventy or eighty more victims might be buried. They, too, had died so that they might serve their ruler in the next world as in this.

The evidence was startling and at first, as Woolley

came upon it, he didn't know what to make of it. Lying side by side in a sloping trench were five men's bodies with daggers at their waists. Farther on were the bodies of ten richly adorned women, arranged in two rows. At the end of the rows lay the ruins of a wonderful harp, and across it the bones of the gold-crowned harpist.

Following the pit along, Woolley came upon a wooden sledge chariot, all turned to dust. In front of it lay the skeletons of two asses. The bodies of the grooms lay at the animals' heads. Close to the chariot was a collection of tools and weapons, among them golden chisels and a big golden saw. Some large stone bowls, copper vessels, and other things were near; then came more human bodies and beyond them a treasure of gold and silver vessels.

Now all this was not in a tomb. It was in a lined open pit that had been dug outside the tomb and afterward covered up. What he was looking at, Woolley realized, were offerings to a dead king or queen!

Another death pit was even more gruesome. The bodies of six men-servants were lined up against the pit wall. In front of them stood a great copper basin, and beside the basin lay the bodies of four women harpists. All the rest of the pit was taken up by the bodies of sixty-four ladies of the court, lying in ordered rows.

Little by little Woolley understood. The burial of a ruler had been a long-drawn-out business. The funeral had not ended when the king or queen had been placed in the tomb. Neither was it over when the few favorite attendants had been killed or drugged and set beside the ruler's bier. When the entrance to the tomb was blocked with stones and brick and plastered over, only the first part of the funeral was completed.

Then followed the unbelievable second part. Down into the open pit, which had been lined with mats, came a rich procession. Soldiers, men-servants, women dressed in all their finery, musicians bearing harps or lyres walked down the ramp into the pit and took their places. Chariots drawn by oxen or by asses were backed down the slope. The drivers stood in the cars, the grooms held the heads of the animals. Last a guard of soldiers formed at the entrance.

The men and women had each brought a little cup of clay or stone or metal, the only thing they would need for the ceremony before them. Some kind of service must have taken place. Anyway the musicians played up to the last. Then each of the victims drank a po-

The musicians played right up to the end of the ceremony.

tion from his cup. What it was, whether drug or poison, Woolley didn't know, but probably it stood ready and waiting for them in a great copper pot in the pit. Then all lay down and composed themselves for death. After a while somebody came down and killed the animals. Perhaps someone else saw to it that everything was in order. Then earth was flung on the unconscious victims. The pit was filled up—and one more royal funeral was over.

XVII

Stephens Starts Something

We began this book in America, and now, having toured Europe, Africa, and Asia, we must go back. For the story of archaeology is incomplete without the New World. Wonderful finds have been made on the twin continents. They have thrown much new light on those First Americans whom we call Indians.

"But didn't we find the Indians just a little while ago?" you may well ask. "Everybody knows what they looked like, how they dressed, made their houses, hunted deer and buffalo, grew corn and beans and pumpkins and squash. The Indians were savages. They were still living in the Stone Age. They fought with bows and arrows and tomahawks—and they scalped their enemies. They could learn to use a gun, but if something went wrong with it, they couldn't fix it. They had no mechanical sense. They never invented the wheel. They had nothing you could call architecture, they knew next to nothing about art, and they had no writing."

A little more than a hundred years ago that's what most people thought. That's the idea most people had about Indians until 1841 when a book called *Incidents of Travel in Central America, Chiapas and Yucatán* came out.

In New York City in the year 1839 there lived a restless young lawyer who had more than the usual bump of curiosity. John L. Stephens had chanced to read a report that strangely excited him. Its author said that in the jungles of Central America and Yucatán there were some very ancient Indian ruins.

Stephens read another account. It said that near Copán, in Honduras, the ruins were well preserved.

But what were they like? Just because the accounts were so vague they stirred Stephens. Here was a

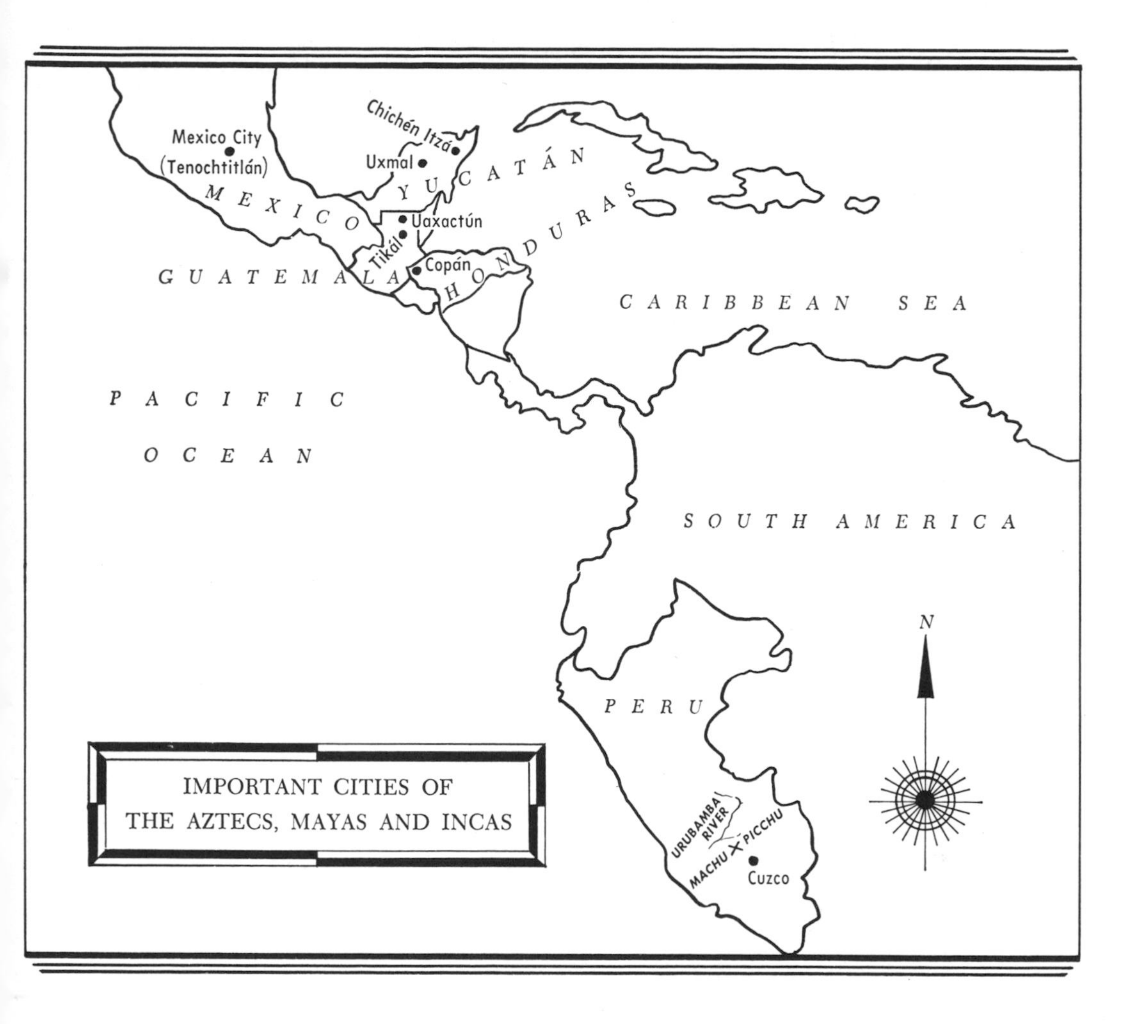

mystery to explore. Architecture in the jungle! Art in the jungle!

He looked up his friend, the English artist Frederick Catherwood. "The world knows almost nothing about these ruins," Stephens said. "They have never been properly sketched or described. It's for you and me to do."

Not many weeks later the two men, mounted on mules, with Indian carriers before and behind, were on the road to Copán. And now they understood why the ruins had never been properly described or sketched. It was as much as a man's life was worth to get to them. Gloomy jungle, steep and narrow mountain passes, mud up to the bellies of the mules—that was the road. Bruised and covered with dirt from head to foot the travelers plodded along. One mishap followed another.

"I would have stayed at home if I had known it would be like this," Catherwood, thrown from his mule, muttered miserably. Stephens, meantime, was thinking: "All we'll get out of this venture is an inscription on our tombstones—'Tossed over the head of a mule, brained by the trunk of a mahogany tree, and buried in the mud of Mico Mountain.' "

But it was over at last. They were in the village of Copán, and now it was a question of plunging into the jungle.

Would they find anything worth all this mighty effort? They went rather hoping than believing. Painfully they followed their guide, who was cutting a way for them with his machete. Suddenly they looked up and gasped. The Indian had brought them to a monument far more wonderful than anything they had dreamed about. They stood staring in utter amazement at the sculptured figure before them. It was of a man curiously and richly dressed. The carving was done in great detail, and the sides of the stone were covered with hieroglyphs.

The friends didn't speak. They merely exchanged a bewildered glance. "This is not the work of savages," that glance said. "This is art, great art." It was a fierce sort of art such as they had never seen and couldn't quite understand. But they recognized it as art of the highest kind.

Already their guide had cut a way to another monument. At the risk of their necks they stumbled to it, then to another and another. When they had looked at fourteen sculptured stones, they turned to a great pyramid that towered above the trees. They climbed up the steep steps, clambered over the flat top, crossed a terrace, went down a flight of steps, up another. Out of breath, they sank down on the edge of a terrace a hundred feet up.

They had to think. They had to get used to this

new idea. History books told them that only savages had lived in America. But after this day they knew better. Savages had never built this pyramid or carved these stones.

But who had done it? Who had built this abandoned city? Their Indian guide, who looked so much like the faces on the sculptured stones, could not tell them. "Who knows?" he said.

Time had done its work. All was forgotten, and neither men nor books could tell them.

They roused themselves. It was frightening to think they were almost the only people on earth who knew anything about this. And there must be many more cities. They couldn't possibly explore all—to do it they would have to cut down the whole jungle. They must be content to rescue a little from forgetfulness. Catherwood must make drawings of the sculptured stones while Stephens explored some more.

Next morning they began. They set Indians to cutting down trees with their machetes so as to let in the light. Then Catherwood put up his drawing board and began to copy. The mosquitoes were so bad he had to work with gloves on.

From Copán the friends traveled on to other forgotten cities. They made notes, plans, sketches. And

The Indian brought them to a wonderful stone monument.

when two years later Stephens' book came out, it created quite a sensation.

Only savages had peopled the New World? Here were Catherwood's drawings to give the lie to that. A people had lived in America who were great architects and artists. They had built beautiful pyramid temples and palaces. They had carved wonderful stone monuments. They had painted pictures. They had invented a hieroglyphic writing.

That was the beginning. Archaeologists and scholars took up from there. It was the Mayan Indians, they said, who had built the abandoned cities. They had been as brilliant a people as any in the Old World. Not only had they invented a hieroglyphic writing. They had invented two kinds of numbers that could be compared to the Roman and the Arabic figures. They had even invented a sign for zero. And they had worked out the most perfect calendar in the world.

Quite likely the scholars and archaeologists would never have learned all this about the Mayas had it not been for a lucky break. They had got hold of a book that had been gathering dust for 300 years in the Royal Academy of Madrid. *Account of Things in Yucatán* proved to be a sort of Rosetta Stone. Diego de Landa, the author, had been the second Bishop of Yucatán. He had done as much as anybody to stamp out Mayan learning by having native books burned as works of the devil. But fortunately he himself had taken pains to learn some of the hieroglyphs. And in his own book he made sketches of them. He sketched the signs for the twenty days of the Mayan month and for the eighteen months of the Mayan year.

Then more breaks came. Three Mayan books turned up in Europe. They must have been taken home by Spanish soldiers. The scholars checked, compared. Slowly they worked out about a third of the signs. The monuments began to speak, and the men in the jungle learned a surprising thing. The Mayas had set up their monuments regularly every twenty years. In the large cities they had set them up every ten or even five years.

A great deal of history became clear then. It was easy to work out the periods when the different cities flourished and when they were abandoned. The puzzling thing was this abandoning. For five or six hundred years the Mayas were caught up in a regular fever of building. It almost seemed as if each great city tried to outdo the others in the size and number of its pyramids and the elaborateness of its monuments. Then suddenly the whole thing went dead. The building boom burst like a bubble. No more pyramids, no more "palaces," no more monuments. Projects were dropped right in the middle. At Uaxactún, the oldest Mayan city yet found, the walls of the latest building were left unfinished. At other sites the last pyramid to go up stopped with the platform—no temple was ever built to crown it. Copán put up its final monument in A.D. 800. Tikál, the largest of the Mayan cities, set up no more after A.D. 869. Uaxactún kept going for another twenty years. And so on.

"What happened?" the archaeologists puzzled. "Why did the Mayas abandon everything they had built with so much hard work?" For a long time they believed that the people of the entire central Mayan region had picked up and gone to Yucatán. They thought so because Mayan history went on from there.

One archaeologist gave it as his opinion that the Mayas were forced to leave on account of their wasteful method of farming. "They depended on maize," he said. "They had to have vast fields of it to support themselves and their priests and nobles. And they had no fertilizer. Their remedy was to burn the trees and bushes on their fields. But every time they burned a field over, they destroyed more of the topsoil. At last the ground was worn out. So they had to move."

But after many years most archaeologists dropped the idea of a wholesale move to Yucatán. "The Mayas stayed right where they were," they said. "They were in their place when the Spaniards came. They are there right now."

"Perhaps," someone suggested, "malaria and yellow fever wiped out such numbers of them that they couldn't keep up the cities any more."

But this theory didn't hold water either. Malaria and yellow fever were almost surely introduced into the New World by the Spaniards, and the Mayan cities had been abandoned centuries before the white men came.

"Maybe a revolt took place," someone else proposed. "Perhaps the priests asked more and more labor of the people so that at last they rose up and overthrew their rulers."

When archaeologists thought of the terrific labor it took to build a single pyramid temple base, they were quite ready to agree that the people must have *wanted* to rebel. But had they actually rebelled? It seemed much more likely that pomp and ceremony had so drugged the Mayas that they remained obedient to the end.

Pomp and ceremony. That was what every archaeologist visualized as he worked around the Mayan cities in the jungle. The cities weren't all alike. But all were planned to dazzle and awe the common people. The temples and so-called "palaces" were raised up on high mounds. They stood together in a sort of towering civic center. Along the fringes, each on its own smaller mound, rose the houses of the priests and nobility. And off at a distance clustered the huts of the farmers, with the maize fields stretching out and out.

"Are they men or gods up on those heights?" the simple farmers must have thought when they came in for the ceremonies. "How brilliant are their feather capes! How gorgeous the quetzal feathers on their heads! How their jeweled armlets glisten in the sun! No, they cannot possibly be people like ourselves. They are gods."

Which, of course, is just what the priests wanted

"Are they men or gods up on those heights?"

them to think. There was no danger of revolt as long as the few remained gods in the eyes of the many. Those Mayan priests were master showmen. They knew that the steep steps of the temple pyramids were just the right setting for pomp and ceremony, and they made the most of every opportunity for stage play. They had plenty of "magic" to show off. They were able astronomers. They could even predict eclipses. They made a magic ceremony out of everything connected with the growing of maize. They knew how to win awe and obedience.

The "unveiling" of a monument must have been a staged ceremony, too. And in this the hieroglyphs themselves surely did their part to keep a distance between the "gods" up on the heights and the people below. For most likely not even the clever sculptors who carved the monuments could read what they so beautifully chiseled. The hieroglyphs were little bits of magic. For the sake of that magic the priests purposely kept the secret of writing from the people.

And that is where they made their mistake. For when king and priests and nobles were swept away by the Spaniards, Mayan civilization vanished too.

How hard it is to make it live again! Archaeologists are trying. In Yucatán the city of Chichén Itzá has been partly cleared. There you can see the Temple of Kukulcan, the Feathered Serpent, patron deity of Chichén Itzá. You can see the Temple of the Warriors, the so-called Observatory, and the great Ball Court where the Mayas played a game something like our basketball. And many other majestic ruins which "pen cannot describe or brush portray."

In Guatemala, Tikál is being rescued from the jungle. Working in the steaming heat, plagued by insects, scorpions, snakes, and vampire bats, archaeologists are freeing Tikál's temples, palaces, monuments, and plazas from the choking jungle growth. Those ruins are but the beautiful dead husks of what was once a living city. Yet even so they give some inkling of the glory that was Maya.

XVIII

When the Spaniards Came

Stephens' book had been an eye opener. People grasped—with a certain pride—that the New World had had a people equal to any in the Old. But more surprises were in store. In 1843 an American scholar by the name of William H. Prescott published *The Conquest of Mexico.* A few years later came his *Conquest of Peru.* He had been burrowing into old Spanish documents and now came up with the results.

To most people it was news to read that the Aztecs had had a vast empire in Mexico and that the Incas had built an even greater one in Peru. People learned with astonishment about temples and palaces, vast armies, roads thousands of miles long, aqueducts, suspension bridges, and fabulous riches of gold, silver, and emeralds.

They read how stunned Cortés and his little band of Spanish adventurers were by their first sight of Tenochtitlán. The Aztec capital of the Emperor Montezuma, with its fifty or more pyramid temples, its aqueduct, causeways, towers, bridges, canals, dikes, lagoons, and floating gardens seemed to them more magnificent than any city they had seen in Europe. A curious crowd had come out to watch the white men and their strange beasts enter the city, and the Spaniards beheld the capital swarming with people.

The sight of the monarch himself was one the adventurers never forgot. From afar they saw Montezuma coming to meet them in a most magnificent litter carried by his chief nobles. A little distance from them, he left the litter and came forward on the arms of four princes. They bore him along under a fringed canopy of the costliest materials, ornamented with green feathers, gold, and precious stones. The king was most richly dressed and adorned. His jeweled buskins were of pure gold. Nobles went before him to spread mantles on the ground lest his feet

As the Spaniards and their strange beasts approached,

should touch it. And except for the four princes, all who attended the monarch kept their eyes fixed upon the earth, not daring to look him in the face.

Had such things really been in America? People read about Mexico and then turned curiously to the story of Peru. They learned with amazement that the Incas had solved the problem of poverty as no other nation in the world had done. In all their land, covering a quarter of South America, there had been no want. Every person was sure of food, clothing, and shelter from birth to death.

And all that vast empire of desert, mountain, and

Montezuma came forth from the city in a magnificent litter.

jungle had been under perfect control. For the Incan kings kept a finger on the pulse of the nation. They had spanned their country with a marvelous system of roads. It covered 10,000 miles. One royal road ran over the lowlands on the edge of the ocean, and another ran over the grand plateau. This last was a miracle of engineering. It went over mountains buried in snow. Galleries were cut through solid rock. Stairways were hewn into the precipices. Deep ravines were filled up with rock. Bridges were suspended over foaming rivers. No uprising could take place anywhere without the news being swiftly carried by runners over the royal roads to the Incan ruler. And at once his armies would be on the march.

People read how fabulous had been the golden wealth of Peru. Not in their wildest dreams had the gold-hungry Spaniards imagined anything like what their eyes beheld. The Temple of the Sun in Cuzco, the Incan capital, was a very mine of gold. The outside of the temple walls was covered with a wide band of plates of gold. Inside, on the western wall, was a golden figure of the Sun with a human face surrounded by rays. It was engraved on an enormous plate of gold powdered with emeralds and precious stones. On either side, on golden thrones, were seated the mummies of former Incan rulers. Gold glowed in burnished plates and studs in every part of the temple. Five fountains threw up sprays of water. The pipes were of gold, the spigots of gold and silver. In the garden outside were plants, animals, birds, and insects —all fashioned out of gold and silver. The very tools used in the temple garden were made of gold.

The greedy Spaniards had plundered Peru. They had subdued Mexico. The Indians had been turned into spiritless slaves—and time had done the rest. Time is a terrible destroyer. Time wipes out even the memory of things.

XIX

Machu Picchu

In the year 1911 Hiram Bingham, a young American historian, was tramping in the Andes looking for Incan ruins. He had come down as head of the Yale Peruvian Expedition, and his project was to find the lost city of Uilcapampa.

What was this Uilcapampa and how had it got lost? To understand what Bingham was looking for we have to go back a moment to the bloody story of Peru.

The Spaniards had captured and executed the Indian ruler Atahualpa. In his stead they had set up another son of the royal Incan line, Manco by name. The conquerors thought that Manco would be a nice, obedient puppet who would make the Incan people submit to them without a fight. But they mistook their man. Manco had spirit. The Inca escaped from the Spaniards, roused his people, and with an army of 200,000 besieged the capital.

The Spaniards all but starved to death in Cuzco. But in the end Manco had to retreat. He withdrew to a mountain fastness and from there made raids on the Spaniards—till he was forced to flee again. He went north over the snowy passes to Uilcapampa. This was a gigantic fortress defended on all sides by Nature, and it could be reached only by fording dangerous torrents or by crossing terribly high mountains. Here the white men could not follow him.

A brawling Spaniard who had taken refuge with the Indians killed the brave Inca Manco. After that Uilcapampa was abandoned and the dead city disappeared from the maps of the Spaniards. It was lost. Even 300 years before Hiram Bingham went down to look for it, no one knew any longer where Manco's refuge had been.

Could the city really have vanished? Hadn't the Incas left any traces in the shape of ruined palaces and temples? Bingham went around asking people if they knew of any ruins. Here and there he picked up vague rumors that led nowhere.

The fiber-cable bridges were great Incan engineering feats.

The explorers had left Cuzco behind them and after some hard travel had entered the canyon of the Urubamba River. Grand scenery was all around them. Great snow peaks loomed above the clouds; granite precipices rose sheer for thousands of feet. Below were the foaming, roaring rapids of the Urubamba.

Twisting around some cliffs, the travelers came suddenly upon a hut. Bingham, as his habit was, asked the owner about ruins. Yes, the peasant answered, there were excellent ones around there. On top of Huayna Picchu, that big mountain just opposite, the gentlemen would find ruins. And also on a ridge of Machu Picchu.

Bingham didn't put much faith in the story. He had been disappointed too many times. But it was his job to investigate all reports of ruins; so they camped, and next morning he arranged to have the peasant guide him up. It was a drizzly day. The naturalist of the expedition looked unfavorably up at the sky and said he would stay in camp. The surgeon decided he had his washing and mending to do. Only the sergeant, whose duty it was to go along, made ready to follow Bingham.

For a stiff three quarters of an hour the two men marched behind the peasant. Then they crossed the Urubamba over a bridge so rude and shaky they had to crawl on hands and knees, after which they began to climb. The way was straight up. They hung on practically by their fingernails, and if not for the ladders that leaned against the worst places of the cliff, they could never have made it at all.

Shortly after noon, they came to a hut. Here, 2,000 feet above the river, two Indian farmers had settled. They gave the travelers gourds of cool water to drink and set cooked sweet potatoes before them. "The ruins are a little farther along," they said.

Bingham wasn't excited. "There will be nothing more interesting up there than the ruins of two or three rude stone houses," he thought. Calmly he sat in the cool shade of the hut enjoying the enchanting view.

At last he rose.

"My son will show you the ruins," one of the farmers said, seeing that the guide wanted to stay and gossip.

At once a small boy sprang forward and eagerly started up the height. Bingham and the sergeant doubtfully followed. It seemed to them they were going up into the clouds. What could be up so high?

They had barely rounded the height, however, when they came on an unexpected sight—a great flight of beautifully made terraces faced with stone. There were hundreds of them, hundreds of feet long. Corn and potatoes and other produce were growing on them. It was clear to Bingham that the farmers below had not built these mountain farms. The terraces were centuries old and had only just been rescued from the jungle. The great trees that had grown up on them lay right where the two Indians had cut them down. The trunks were too heavy to lug away.

Who built these terraces? Bingham wondered. Still, he wasn't unduly excited—he had seen such things before. Patiently he followed the boy. Then suddenly the explorer found himself looking at the walls of ruined houses. The stonework was beautiful, the best; he had never seen any better. The stones were most carefully cut and perfectly fitted together.

The boy had gone on and, scrambling after him through dense undergrowth, the two men came without any warning upon a cave lined with the finest cut stone. Bingham recognized that this had been a royal tomb. Above it was an overhanging ledge, and on top of the ledge a building. Its outer wall was slightly curved and gently sloping. The shape reminded him strongly of the Temple of the Sun in Cuzco. Was this also a Temple of the Sun? Another wall tied into it, and this, too, was clearly the work of a master hand. The stones were so beautifully fitted together that no mortar was needed to hold them in place. The white granite rocks looked as if they had *grown* together.

Beautifully made terraces covered the mountainside.

"No wall in Cuzco is as beautiful as this," Bingham thought, staring at it in unbelief. It seemed like a dream. The wall and the temple fairly took his breath away. Dimly he realized that he was looking at stonework as fine as the finest in the world.

"What can this place be?" he asked himself. "Why has no one given us an idea of it? But perhaps," he thought, "this is just a small place off by itself. Perhaps it has escaped notice because it is so out of the way and hard to get to."

"Up here!" the boy called.

Tearing himself away, Bingham, with the sergeant treading on his heels, climbed up a steep hill over what seemed to be a flight of stone steps. And now surprise followed on bewildering surprise. First they came to a great stairway of large granite blocks. Crossing a clearing where the farmers had planted a small vegetable garden, they suddenly found themselves standing in front of what Bingham recognized as the finest and most interesting ruins in ancient America. Each building had only three walls—the fourth side was open to let the sun stream in. There were niches in the wall. Against the back wall under the niches was a great stone block fourteen feet long. It might be an altar, Bingham thought. Or perhaps it was the throne on which the mummies of departed Incas had been set out to be worshiped.

Spellbound he stood there. The buildings were made of the same beautiful white granite, and the stones in the lower tier were higher than a man. "Each one of these blocks weighs ten to fifteen tons," passed through the explorer's mind. "How ever did the Incas bring them here and set them up and fit them so perfectly when all they had to work with was stone hammers and little bronze crowbars? Will anyone believe what I have found?"

The temple faced a plaza or courtyard. Bingham turned to look at it, caught a glimpse of something and gasped. On the east side of the plaza stood the ruins of another temple, and in the wall of that temple were *three great windows* looking to the rising sun. Never had he seen anything like this in Peru. There *was* nothing like it. But he had read about just such a building as this. Three hundred years ago a descendant of the Incas had written about the ancient things of Peru. In his book he had said that the first Inca, Manco the Great, had ordered "a masonry wall with three windows" to be built at the place of his birth.

"Is this what I have found?" Bingham asked himself. "Is this the birthplace of the first Inca? Or can this place be Uilcapampa, the fortress of the last Inca, the refuge to which Manco fled?"

In that first wild moment he could not make up his mind. Later Bingham let himself believe he had found both. But when it came to naming his find, he let soberness rule. The ruins lay on a narrow bridge between Machu Picchu and Huayna Picchu. He called the unknown city *Machu Picchu.*

Machu Picchu it has remained—this breath-taking fortress of the Incas, which the curious from all over the world travel thousands of miles to see. It was not Uilcapampa—we know that now. Machu Picchu was just the last of a chain of "hanging cities" which the Incas built on the heights. But its wonder is none the less for that. There it stands just as the last inhabitants left it, only that the thatched roofs are gone. There it stands with its temples and palaces and houses, its plazas and its endless flights of steps—4,000 feet above the roaring rapids of the Urubamba and 10,000 feet above the sea. A city in the clouds. An eagle's eyrie.

XX

There Is No End

Bat Cave is a large rock shelter in New Mexico. The waves of glacial Lake San Augustin pounded that cave out of the rock. The lake is gone now. It vanished a long time ago, and the area is nothing but barren flats today.

In the 1940's Herbert W. Dick, working for Harvard University, dug into the floor of Bat Cave. Indians had lived in it—that was clear to see. As long as 6,000 years ago they had taken over the cave. For Dick found their flints in a level of deposits which geologists said was as old as that. But the exciting thing was that somewhere along the line the inhabitants of Bat Cave had started using maize. There the evidence was—kernels of corn and tiny curled and dried-up cobs.

The maize was both a pod and a popcorn and different from any ever found before. It was far more primitive. The tiny cobs weren't enclosed in husks as we know corn to be. The husks stood out around the base like the calyx of a flower. And each kernel of corn had a small leaf covering all its own.

The cobs kept getting smaller as Dick dug down till at last there were no more. "How old can this maize be?" he wondered.

Now Dick himself couldn't give an exact answer. But science could. It has figured out a way of finding out how old anything is—if it was once alive. Science can tell from the amount of Carbon 14 left in the material. For as long as something is alive, it has a definite, unchanging amount of Carbon 14. But as soon as it dies, it starts losing this Carbon 14 at a steady, known rate.

The Carbon 14 test said the cobs and kernels in the middle levels of Bat Cave were 2,800 years old. That made the maize in the earliest levels of the layer at least 4,000 years old!

Now up to this time there had been no proof that the Indians had done any farming before the year 1.

Here was the proof. The maize in Bat Cave showed that Indians had been growing corn 2,000 years before the year 1. They were growing it when the palace of Minos first rose in Crete—and even earlier—for maize certainly wasn't born in New Mexico. All evidence pointed south, perhaps as far south as northern South America, and it had probably taken maize some time to travel up.

That Indians were farmers long before the Trojan War is just one of a thousand fascinating things archaeologists have learned about them since Stephens and Catherwood rode their mules into Copán. In the 1890s, in a shallow cave in Grand Gulch, Utah, four young ranchboys discovered ancient skeletons. The flesh was dried on them as on a mummy. Over the head of each was a huge basket. Beside every body was a pair of sandals with square toes. Archaeologists came down to study the Basket Makers, as the boys called them. And out of the dark rose the Anasazi—the Ancient Ones. They had lived in the desert perhaps 2,000 years before Columbus sailed. Here were their baskets of yucca fiber. Here were their sandals of yucca cord, their blankets of rabbit fur, their traps made of yucca fiber and human hair.

In Chaco Canyon, New Mexico, archaeologists have

explored twelve great apartment houses built on the heights by the early Pueblos. The largest of these houses is Pueblo Bonito. It is a whole town. It covers three acres of ground and has at least 800 rooms. Once it housed perhaps 1,200 people. The Indians built it about the time the Norsemen discovered America. It was the largest apartment house in the world till the year 1882, when a bigger one was built in New York.

All over the eastern United States there are man-made hills. From the Mississippi to the Appalachians those mounds lie—maybe 100,000 of them. They are of various shapes and sizes, and they seem to have been built for different purposes. Some were fortifications, some bases for temples, and some burial places. Many experts think that the builders of these mounds were not ancestors of the Indians found in the region by the first white men. The things discovered in the mounds indicate that many of the people who built the mounds had a more advanced civilization than the later Indians. Archaeologists have found copper knives and spear points in the mounds. They have also found tools made of iron taken from meteorites, as well as silver and gold worked in the same way as copper. The search is still going on, for much remains to be learned about these mysterious early Americans.

In Mexico the great pyramids of the Aztecs and of still earlier peoples, on whose shoulders the Aztecs stood as the Romans stood on the shoulders of the Etruscans, have been uncovered. In Peru archaeologists have explored the royal roads of the Incas. There is no end to archaeology in the Americas. In a hundred places on the two continents men and women are digging up the story of the American Indian, whose talents were so long misjudged. Not everyone can have the glory of finding a lost and forgotten city. But humbler things sometimes have even more to say to us. In 1944 little wheeled toys made of pottery were dug up near Tampico in Mexico. They were pull-toys. The little clay dogs had their legs pierced for a slender rod to go through, and on the ends of each rod pottery wheels were jammed.

What wonderful meaning there is for us in those small wheeled toys! A little more time and perhaps the wheel would have been put to other uses, though those early Americans had no animal that could drag a cart. A little more time and the Aztecs would surely have worked out real writing. They were just on the verge. If they had been left alone, what might not Indians have achieved!

Index

Index

SPACE SCIENCE

All About Satellites and Space Ships
by David Dietz

All About Rockets and Jets
by Fletcher Pratt

All About the Planets
by Patricia Lauber

All About the Stars
by Anne Terry White

PHYSICAL SCIENCE

All About the Atom
by Ira M. Freeman

All About Electricity
by Ira M. Freeman

All About Radio and Television
by Jack Gould

All About Engines and Power
by Sam and Beryl Epstein

All About the Wonders of Chemistry
by Ira M. Freeman

All About Sound and Ultrasonics
by Ira M. Freeman

PHYSIOLOGY AND MEDICINE

All About the Human Body
by Bernard Glemser

All About Great Medical Discoveries
by David Dietz

GREAT DISCOVERIES

All About Archaeology
by Anne Terry White

All About Prehistoric Cave Men
by Sam and Beryl Epstein

All About Famous Scientific Expeditions
by Raymond P. Holden

All About Famous Inventors and Their Inventions
by Fletcher Pratt

THE UNITED STATES

All About Our 50 States
by Margaret Ronan

All About the U.S. Navy
by Edmund L. Castillo

MUSIC

All About the Symphony Orchestra
by Dorothy Berliner Commins

EARTH SCIENCE

All About the Planet Earth
by Patricia Lauber

All About Mountains and Mountaineering
by Anne Terry White

All About Volcanoes and Earthquakes
by Frederick H. Pough

All About Our Changing Rocks
by Anne Terry White

All About the Ice Age
by Patricia Lauber

All About the Weather
by Ivan Ray Tannehill

All About the Sea
by Ferdinand C. Lane

All About Sailing the Seven Seas
by Ruth Brindze

All About Undersea Exploration
by Ruth Brindze

All About Great Rivers of the World
by Anne Terry White

All About the Jungle
by Armstrong Sperry

All About the Desert
by Sam and Beryl Epstein

All About the Arctic and Antarctic
by Armstrong Sperry

NATURAL SCIENCE

All About Animals and Their Young
by Robert M. McClung

All About Horses
by Marguerite Henry

All About Dogs
by Carl Burger

All About Monkeys
by Robert S. Lemmon

All About Whales
by Roy Chapman Andrews

All About Fish
by Carl Burger

All About Birds
by Robert S. Lemmon

All About the Insect World
by Ferdinand C. Lane

All About Moths and Butterflies
by Robert S. Lemmon

All About Snakes
by Bessie M. Hecht

All About Dinosaurs
by Roy Chapman Andrews

All About Strange Beasts of the Past
by Roy Chapman Andrews

All About Strange Beasts of the Present
by Robert S. Lemmon

All About the Flowering World
by Ferdinand C. Lane